**This book is to be returned on or before
the last date stamped below.** 362-67

LIBREX

KRAM

DOMESTIC VIOLENCE

VIOLENCE

The Circle Called Love

Sue W. Kramer

To order additional copies of this book, contact:
Xlibris Corporation
1-888-7-XLIBRIS
www.Xlibris.com
Orders@Xlibris.com

CONTENTS

This book is dedicated to the victims of domestic violence. May you find knowledge, strength, and the courage to leave within these pages.

INTRODUCTION

I am not an expert on domestic violence. "Domestic Violence: The Circle Called Love" is the result of months spent pouring through the Lambertville Police Department's domestic violence case files, compiling and evaluating statistics, accumulating research, and interpreting the behaviors of abusers.

I am also not a police officer, social worker, or other professional who works in close contact with domestic violence, its victims, or its abusers.

When I entered Trenton State College in 1965, I had my mind set on becoming a professional musician. Until that point, music had been my life and I was fairly adept at playing the tenor sax and string bass. I had been in the marching band, band, orchestra, and dance band throughout high school, and had even cut a record as part of my summer music program at the University of Vermont, played by invitation at McCarter Theater in Princeton, and studied under the director of the Royal Thai Air Force Band in Bangkok, Thailand.

So, it was a surprise to not only myself, but everyone who knew me when I suddenly switched my major to special education after attending an exceptional college presentation.

Throughout college, I was a strong writer, but as I approached my senior year, I realized that my "true calling" was in the area of criminal investigation. Abnormal psychology and violent crime fascinated me, and the more I read and learned, the more I wanted to know what made the violent offender "tick."

I decided to continue my formal education in that area, with the hopes of establishing a career as an investigator with either the F.B.I. or the New Jersey State Police.

Things didn't work out quite as I planned, and with a BA in education, I went into teaching, and wound up with ulcers rather than my dreamed of career in law enforcement.

By the mid '90s, and after several job changes, I found myself living in Lambertville, NJ with my husband Frank, running Harry K. Kramer & Son, a successful retail cemetery memorial business.

By then, I had been talking about writing and crime for nearly 30 years and I realized it was time to do something about it or stop talking. I decided to start writing.

I had just completed my first novel, "Madison," and was trying to find a literary agent to represent me when I discovered Knowledge Solutions, LLC, and Brent E. Turvey, a man whom my husband refers to as "the other man in my life."

Brent, whom I greatly respect not only as a teacher, but as an internationally known criminal profiler, forensics expert, and criminal investigator, guided me through my first course on criminal profiling, opening my eyes to evidence based behavioral profiling and whetting my appetite for more.

About the same time, our city on the Delaware River was undergoing major changes in its police department. After several embattled years, Lambertville abolished the position of police chief in favor of hiring a police director.

The man who was chosen to fill this newly created position was a retired Hamilton Township deputy police chief named Al Varga.

One of the first things Al did was start a Crime Watch program. After the first meeting, he casually mentioned that he was looking for volunteers to write the police department's press releases.

I jumped at the opportunity. Writing the press releases for the police department seemed to be a natural extension of my interests.

And, I continued studying-and learning about psychopaths, rape investigation, homicide investigation, forensics, and evidence based behavioral profiling. Along the way, I found out that Al was a graduate of the FBI's criminal profiling program, and had in fact, studied under the infamous profiling team of Robert Ressler and John Douglas.

My continuing education and training, love of writing, and time spent volunteering at police headquarters came together one day when Al and I were talking and he told me that Lambertville had the highest per capita rate of domestic violence in Hunterdon County. Then, he asked me if I would be willing to work on a project for the department-to profile the abuser in an attempt to get to the heart and soul of domestic violence and define what was really happening in these sometimes-fatal relationships.

What a unique concept, profiling the abuser! Little did I know how that idea would change my life.

I got to work, and three months later handed Al the finished project. After he read it, he encouraged me to find a way to publish it.

Our local newspaper, The Beacon, a Packet Publication, picked up my domestic violence study and ran it as a series in the fall of 1998. To my surprise, my editor, Mae Rhine, submitted the series to the New Jersey Press Association competition, and it won first place in the area of Public Service, the coveted Lloyd P. Burns Memorial Award.

Mae asked me to write another series the following year, another award winner on drug abuse, and then one day she called out of the blue-she needed someone to cover a breaking story and asked me to do it.

I did it, and I've been writing steadily for The Beacon ever since. And people are still calling me to ask for copies of my domestic violence series.

The original series has touched and saved lives around the country. Armed with the understanding of what was happening in their abusive relationships, victims have found the courage to leave their abuser and start a new life.

"Domestic Violence: The Circle Called Love" has as its basis, my domestic violence series. I have added some new information and expanded other areas in response to the many requests I've had for more case stories.

I must thank Brent E. Turvey for recognizing the need for professional education and training in the areas of evidence based behavioral profiling and criminal investigation in general-not just for people in all levels of law enforcement and the criminal justice system, but others, such as myself, who are simply eager to learn. He gave me the mental tools I needed to carry out this project, and more.

I must thank Al Varga, for his encouragement and support. Without his faith in my abilities, none of this would have happened. He stands behind me, not only with "Domestic Violence: The Circle Called Love," but my novels, "Madison" and "Lynette."

Mae Rhine, my editor, is also deserving of my thanks. It was she who had enough faith in me and my writing to go out on a limb and publish the original domestic violence series. And, she keeps me busy every day, covering breaking news, writing feature articles, and doing investigative stories.

There is one other person who is the unsung hero in all this, my husband, Frank. Without his love and support, none of this would be possible. He has lovingly supported me as I worked late into the evening, laughed when I was so involved in my work that I forgot to make dinner, and never complained when my computer went on vacation with us.

Above and beyond this, I want everyone to know that our relationship is a loving and caring one. Frank is a kind and gentle man who supports me in everything I do; and I support him in all that he does.

My wish for everyone in a violent relationship is that they find the courage to leave and ultimately find the kind of love I've found with Frank.

Sue W. Kramer

SUE W. KRAMER IS AN AFFILIATE MEMBER IN THE GENERAL SECTION OF THE *Academy of Behavioral Profiling.* The Academy is a professional association dedicated to the application of evidence based criminal profiling techniques within investigative and legal venues.

Sue's website is http://www.suewkramer.com/

PROLOGUE

Who among us can ever forget the picture of Nicole Brown Simpson that flashed across television screens worldwide-her face swollen, discolored, and battered-the result of an argument with her husband; an argument that had escalated into a brutal beating.

Nicole wanted things to change. She tried to make the violence stop. But, it didn't. And, for all of the other men, women and children who are the battered and abused victims of domestic violence, things probably won't change either.

If anything, the situation will become worse. Many will suffer in silence. Sometimes, the victim will wind up in the hospital, as did a Lambertville woman who was choked and beaten so severely by her husband that she miscarried their unborn baby. (Kramer, Victim, 1998) She was only one of the approximately 1.4 million people who require medical treatment each year for injuries caused by domestic violence. (Rand, 1997)

Sometimes, the victims are forced into hiding to escape the attempted stranglings, shooting, beatings, and threats. And, if past statistics hold true, 1,800 people will die this year-murdered, in the name of love. (U.S. DOJ, Press, 1998)

What is this thing we call domestic violence? How does it happen? Who are the batters? The victims? And, what exactly is the violent circle called love? The answers can be surprising.

Although many of the examples and the statistics given are from Hunterdon County and Lambertville in New Jersey, no community escapes domestic violence, and the reader should understand that although the statistics for their community may be slightly different, they are still there.

It is hoped that "Domestic Violence: The Circle Called Love" will not only enhance the understanding of domestic violence within professional circles, but help the lay person, and the victims of domestic violence in particular, recognize the inherent truths that shape abusive relationships.

This book is dedicated to the men, women, and children who have been, are, and will become the victims of domestic violence, with the hope that they will come to understand that they don't have to stay in an abusive or violent relationship. They are good and worthwhile people who can have a wonderful, sunny future ahead of them, free of violence and abuse.

CHAPTER 1

Domestic violence is a crime. It is shoving, hitting, punching, beating, kicking, choking-any type of physical contact made in anger by an intimate. It can be a single shove, a brutal beating, or murder. It is the physical abuse of one intimate by another and can run the gamut from a single slap to enslavement and physical torture.

And, physical abuse has another side-emotional abuse. Emotional abuse can be subtle, nothing more than degrading or humiliating comments made by one partner directed against the other. It can sneak up on the victim, slowly growing until the victim finds them self under the complete control of another, being told what they can and can not do, stripped of all dignity, and emotionally broken.

Domestic violence doesn't always stay behind closed doors, limiting itself to emotional abuse or beatings, either. It includes a wide range of criminal offenses that include harassment, criminal trespassing, burglary, criminal mischief, lewdness, criminal sexual contact, sexual assault, false imprisonment, criminal restraint, kidnapping, terroristic threats, assault, stalking, and homicide. There were 85,018 domestic violence offenses reported to New Jersey police departments in these categories alone in 1996. Of those, 43,017 were assaults, 30,191 were harassment complaints, 353 were stalking incidents, and 43 were homicides. (New Jersey State Police, 1996, 189)

Domestic violence occurs between husbands and wives, parents and children, boyfriends and girlfriends, former partners and live-ins. No distinction is made between male/female, adult/child, or heterosexual/homosexual; all these relationships are affected and anyone can become a victim. And surprisingly, the majority of victims of domestic violence aren't women.

Domestic violence cases like the 1998 murder/suicide that took the life of television star Phil Hartman, with the female partner being the aggressor, aren't unusual. Male victims are just more reluctant to disclose the fact that they are being abused than women.

In our culture, men have been traditionally viewed as being emotionally stronger than women. They are raised on the premise that it's not all right to cry. As children, they are told, "Be a man . . . don't come home crying . . . you're acting like a baby." They are taught at an early age that they must learn to control their emotions, be strong, and assume the role of provider and protector in a relationship. Conventionally raised men then, tend to view abuse by a woman as putting them in a non-masculine role. They keep their emotions in check, take the abuse, and don't talk about it. When the issue of spousal battery being initiated by the woman is brought to light, as in the case of Phil Hartman, it very often isn't addressed fully in the media or domestic violence studies.

Murray A. Strouse, the co-director of the Family Research Laboratory at the University of New Hampshire, puts the blame for the lack of publicity about male abuse solely on women in the battered women's shelter movement for denying or playing down women's roles in the physical abuse of their intimates. He goes on to say that in a recent national Canadian study, the data on women abusing men was left out because it was considered to be "politically embarrassing." (Price, 1994) Others agree that there is a problem in reporting the abuse of men by women. In a special supplement to the Washington Post, Armin A. Brott (1993) reports incidents of authors being threatened with violence, economic sanctions, or denounced for publishing works about women abusing men. Cathy Young, a newspaper columnist and author of the book *Gender Wars*, goes one step further when she says studies show that "women not only hit as often as men, but they usually land the first punch." (1998)

In fact, a 1985 National Family Violence Survey found that women initiated assaults on their husbands in 124 of 1,000 couples, while men were the aggressors in only 122 of 1,000 couples. Women led men as the aggressor in minor assaults also, with women being the responsible party in 78 couples out of 1,000 and men in only 72 out of 1,000. Men only surpassed the rate for women in the area of severe assaults, with 50 assaults per 1,000 couples initiated by men and 46 per 1,000 couples initiated by women. (Price, 1994)

Domestic violence knows no boundaries. Foreign-born women are particularly susceptible as victims. Often, they have been raised in a culture that accepts domestic abuse and female subservience and they may be under the impression that United States laws and protective services don't apply to them. When a woman in this type of situation tries to leave, she is also faced with a language barrier, which can be an almost insurmountable hurdle. She then finds herself isolated by her heritage; unaware of her rights in the United States, unable to find a bilingual shelter, unable to obtain financial assistance, and afraid of the legal system. (Orloff, et. al., 133, 1995)

Gay and Lesbian victims of domestic violence also face extra hurdles. While the type and prevalence of reported abuse is the same as in heterosexual relationships, victims of same-sex battery receive fewer government and legal protections. Seven states define domestic violence as a heterosexual crime, leaving Gay and Lesbian victims with no legal recourse. (Barnes, 1998) As same-sex victims, they are denied services and protection at many of the 1500 shelters and safe houses across the country. (Murphy, 1995) And, in 21 states, there are sodomy laws, which force Gay and Lesbian victims to confess to a crime in order to prove the existence of a domestic relationship! (Barnes, 1998)

Domestic violence spills over into the workplace, too. Up to 50% of abuse victims report interference with their attempts to sustain employment or continue their education. Abusers make repeated phone calls to the workplace, even calling the employer, demanding the victim quit. They make false allegations against the victim, forcing him or her to take time off to appear in court or report to social services. They have made death threats, and have even gone to the workplace to commit suicide in front of the victim. Women are beaten up on their way to interviews, stalked, have their writing arms repeatedly broken, find their cars vandalized, work clothes missing, and are abused as they are leaving for work. (American Bar Association, Raphael, 10-14, 1997)

Domestic violence statistics for the United States, as compiled by the Federal Bureau of Investigation and Bureau of Justice paint a horrifying picture of the scope of abuse in our society.

- 97% of all *reported* domestic violence victims are women.
- 61% of child abuse is perpetrated by women. (Woodworth, 1998)
- Domestic violence injures more women than rapes, muggings, and automobile accidents combined and is the leading cause of injury to women between the ages of 15 and 45.
- 17% of the people treated in emergency rooms are injured by a spouse, former spouse, boyfriend, or girlfriend. (Barnes, 1998, 25)
- As many as 33% of all Gay and Lesbian relationships are violent. (Barnes, 1998, 25)
- As many as 100,000 Lesbians and 500,000 Gay men are battered each year. (Murphy, 1995)
- In 1996, 2,600 people in New Jersey over the age of 60 were victims of domestic violence. (NJSP, 198)
- Assaults accounted for 39% of those offenses against the New Jersey elderly in 1996, with a total of 1,023 victims. (NJSP, 198)
- There were 371 violent domestic offenses *reported* in Hunterdon County in 1994. Of those, 180 were assaulted and one person was killed. This represents a 10% increase over 1993 (NJSP, 1994, 5,6)

- The *reported* incidents of domestic violence continue to rise in Hunterdon County, with 450 reported cases in 1995 and 468 cases reported in 1996. Those figures represent a 4% increase. (NJSP, 1996, 190,191)
- Lambertville has the highest per capita rate of domestic violence in Hunterdon County. In the first six months of 1998 alone, there were 18 cases of domestic violence reported to the police. (Lambertville Police Department, 1998)
- Other domestically related offenses such as harassment, assaults, breaking and entering, criminal mischief, and sexual assault bring the total number of reported domestic violence crimes for the first half of 1998 to 40. (Lambertville Police Department, 1998)
- With only one seventh of all domestic violence incidents being reported to the police, (Florida Governors Task Force, 1997, 3) the actual number of domestic violence incidents occurring in Lambertville during the first half of 1998 can be more realistically calculated to be 280.
- That means that Lambertville, with a population of 4,285 has approximately 3 domestic violence incidents every two days, 47 per month, and 560 yearly.

Domestic violence is a crime. It can affect anyone and any relationship. It transcends the boundaries of race, religion, sexual preference, and culture. It can affect every aspect of the victim's life from their home environment to their job. And for many, domestic violence is a cruel trap that is perpetuated by antiquated laws, prejudiced victim assistance services, and the restrictions of foreign cultures.

CHAPTER 2

In order to recognize and understand the true dynamics of domestic violence, we must first identify the characteristics that distinguish a healthy loving relationship from an abusive and violent one.

A healthy relationship is a partnership where the couple makes joint decisions and share in the responsibilities. They openly discuss work, school and money issues without yelling or violence. They share their innermost feelings and respond to each other's needs just as easily as they share their money and possessions. The loving couple respects each other and each other's opinions-in and out of the bedroom. They listen, understand, and trust. (Boston University Medical Center, 1995-1996)

The abusive relationship, on the other hand, is a master/servant relationship where the abuser makes the decisions. The abusive partner denies job freedom, money, and personal freedom. The abusive partner uses domination, intimidation, manipulation, and control tactics to get their way. (BUMC)

These tactics-and the abuse-carry over into the bedroom. One out of every three women in a violent relationship is raped by their intimates. In many of these cases, a weapon is used. (MNPD, 1996)

The Boston University Medical Center has identified specific behaviors that occur during abuse. (1995-1996) The first set of behaviors that have been identified are *emotionally abusive* behaviors.

- Verbal Abuse-Name-calling, blaming, yelling, swearing, and making humiliating remarks or gestures.

- Pressure Tactics-Rushing you to make decisions, making you feel guilty, intimidation, sulking, not talking, threatening to withhold money, and manipulating the children.
- Abuse of Authority-Telling you what to do, always claiming to be right, making big decisions, using "logic" to make you "wrong," and insisting their statements are "the truth."
- Disrespect-Interrupting you, ignoring or not responding to you, changing topics, twisting your words, belittling you in front of others, and saying bad things about your friends and family.
- Abusing Trust-Lying, being secretive, withholding information, cheating on you, and being overly jealous.
- Breaking Promises-Not following through on agreements, not sharing in responsibilities of the household and childcare, and letting you down.
- Emotional Withholding-Not telling you how they feel about things, not giving you emotional support, not giving you attention, not complimenting you, showing no respect for your feelings, rights, or opinions.
- Blaming/Denying-Making light of their behavior, not taking your concerns about their behavior seriously, denying the abuse happened, blaming you or someone else for their abusive behavior.
- Economic Control-Interfering with your job. Not letting you get a job. Refusing to give you money. Taking your money, taking your car keys, preventing you from using the car or driving, and threatening to report you to welfare, DYFS, or other social service agencies.
- Self-Destructive Behavior-Abusing drugs or alcohol, threatening suicide or other types of harm, and deliberately doing things that will have negative results.
- Isolation-Preventing you from or making it difficult for you to see friends and family, monitoring phone calls, and telling you where you can or cannot go.

- Harassment-Making uninvited visits or calls, following you, checking up on you, embarrassing you in public, and refusing to leave when asked.

The next set of abuser behaviors are acts of violence. These behaviors are not just signs of a violent, abusive relationship, they are *the defining elements of a violently abusive relationship*, and any one of these behaviors is abuse. (BUMC)

- Intimidation-Making angry or threatening gestures, use of physical size to intimidate, blocking the doorway during arguments, out-shouting you, and driving recklessly.
- Destruction-Destroying your possessions, punching walls, and throwing and/or breaking things.
- Threats-Making and/or carrying out threats to hurt you or others.
- Sexual Violence-Degrading treatment during sex and using force, threats, or coercion to get you to agree to sex or perform sexual acts.
- Physical Violence-Slapping, punching, grabbing, kicking, choking, pushing, biting, burning, stabbing, and/or shooting you, your children, or your pets.
- Weapons-Use of weapons, keeping weapons around which frighten you, threatening or attempting to kill you or those you love, and/or carrying out any threats to hurt you or others.

As though these violent behaviors weren't frightening enough, it should be understood that nearly 100% of the offenders who verbally abuse, hit or throw objects, break objects or make threats, progress to physically assaulting/battering their victim. They begin by pushing, grabbing, or restraining the victim. The next level of violence includes more physical behaviors such as slapping, kicking, pinching, and pulling out clumps of hair. The most severe levels of violence can include choking, beating the victim with objects and the use of weapons. (MNPD, 1996)

The signs and behaviors of domestic violence and abuse can be subtle and may begin to appear in the "dating" stage of a relationship when the victim is asked to stop wearing makeup, comb their hair differently, dress differently, or stop seeing friends and family.

The abuser might call the victim names, lie about what they're doing or where they've been, or constantly check on the victim's whereabouts by phoning the victim's work, school, or home.

No matter how the abuse manifests itself, it is not the basis of a loving, caring, and sharing relationship; it is a crime, and the abuse and control will only become worse over time.

CHAPTER 3

For a clear understanding of how these behaviors manifest themselves in a violent relationship, and to then understand what the behaviors mean, we have to take a detailed look at the interdependence of the abuser and victim; we have to define their relationship to each other and then examine the behaviors in light of that relationship. We have to look at domestic violence from all viewpoints, from that of law enforcement to victim to abuser in order to obtain the total picture.

Five victims, each with different histories of abuse and different levels of violence, shared their stories for this book. Their names and some identifying factors were changed to protect the identity of the victims.

*   *   *

Sally, a Lambertville resident, battered wife, and mother of four small children, spent every Sunday evening at a church social gathering. This small bit of freedom was just about the only considerate thing her husband Alex ever did for her. And, while Sally was at church, Alex watched the children.

Alex always yelled at Sally when she got home and very often his verbal abuse turned into a beating. Sally was accused of many things Sunday nights, including cheating on him, and being a poor wife and mother. Alex said he couldn't cope with the children, and said the abuse and beatings were all Sally's fault because she was gone so long for her own selfish needs.

What was actually happening every Sunday evening? In reality, Alex was sexually molesting his children while Sally was in church. When confronted with this, Alex merely shrugged it off and said, "So what? It was nothing. Let it go, and forget about it." (Kramer, Victim, 1998)

*   *   *

Bunny, another Lambertville resident, met Sam at a church singles gathering in 1984. Sam was a handsome, charming, considerate, and attentive partner, the man of Bunny's dreams. After dating a short time, the two rented a home together. Bunny settled blissfully into the relationship, more than willing to do anything to please her partner. Sam was also happy in the relationship, although he preferred locking himself in the den to watch movies while Bunny entertained. Bunny reasoned that he was tired-after all, Sam worked hard all week.

Sometimes, Sam worked in the yard while Bunny entertained, a sign Bunny was sure, that he took pride in their property. A year or so into the relationship, Sam kindly told Bunny, who he was now calling by her formal name of Bernadette, that he really preferred Chinese food to her cooking. He started getting take-out every night, never missing an opportunity to throw Bunny's home cooked meals into the garbage.

Sam lost his job. He said his boss was unbearable to work for, had ties to organized crime, kept loaded guns in the office, and had forced him to quit his job out of fear.

In reality, Sam was fired from his job after repeatedly not showing up for work.

Then, Sam bought a computer. He spent so many hours writing resumes and researching job opportunities that he no longer had time to work in the yard or help around the house. But, Bunny didn't mind doing all of the work. She maintained that Sam was a gem, a one in a million kind of guy. He started openly drinking great quantities of alcohol, confirming Bunny's suspicions that he had been secretly drinking. But, then again, Bunny reasoned, he was really stressed out from spending all day at the computer.

What was Sam really doing on the computer? While Bunny worked, he was in Internet "chat rooms," actively soliciting women to partake in the sexual fantasy scenarios he had created.

Over time, Sam increased his verbal assaults on Bunny. He called her names and belittled her at every chance. He refused to take her anywhere and let no one in the house. He was on the computer day and night. He bought Chinese food, videos, VCRs, televisions, computer games, collectibles and drank. In all, Sam charged over $100,000 on his credit cards.

It didn't matter when Sam's car broke down, because he wasn't working anyway. But, Bunny continued to feel sorry for Sam. She reasoned that he was so smart that he was overqualified for the jobs he applied for and the stress he was under was almost unbearable.

Then, in one of his drunken rages, Sam destroyed half the house, smashing dishes, throwing things, and threatening Bunny. Later that night, he urinated on the carpet, ordering Bunny to clean up the mess, an event that was repeated every night thereafter.

Bunny suffered in silence as things worsened, putting on a smiling front during the day and enduring Sam's drunken rages and forced sex at night. Although Bunny didn't realize it, Sam was drinking all day as he sat at the computer. He had an extensive collection of Internet pornography and was placing "want ads," still in search of his fantasy sexual partner.

By now, Sam was openly talking about his fantasy sexual scenarios and telling Bunny about his "ideal partner," who would be nothing like her. He would sit at the computer and drink long after Bunny went to bed at night and he always woke Bunny out of a sound sleep to launch his drunken sexual attacks. Sam would routinely stop in the middle of their "lovemaking" for a drink and cigarettes. His sexual performance, inhibited by the alcohol, very often reduced him to rages in which he would cry, threaten Bunny, and detail ways in which he would take his own life. He would spend hours lamenting on his "problems," placing the blame for all his problems directly on others and keeping Bunny awake for hours on end.

When things finally became intolerable for her, and in fear of her life, Bunny threw some of her belongings into her car and left. In all the years of abuse, Bunny never called the police or admitted to anyone that Sam beat her. (Kramer, Victim, 1998)

*   *   *

Another Lambertville woman, Tippi met A.H. through their mutual work with a charitable organization. He was tall, dark, handsome, and charming. After a whirlwind romance, they married. Tippi lived in a state of bliss for just one month before the abuse began.

A.H. was methodical and predictable in his attacks on his wife. Demanding perfection, he held "white glove" inspections of their apartment and everything, including defrosting the freezer, was done at his direction and to his satisfaction. Tippi was required to have a full meal waiting on the table at precisely midnight each night, a meal in which A.H. measured Tippi's portions, never allowing her a second helping. She was not allowed to drive the car or even renew her license.

A.H. maintained total control over Tippi, launching into verbal abuse if he found anything not to his liking or discovered any attempts to break any of his rules. And, according to A.H., Tippi never did anything right. She couldn't cook or clean to his satisfaction. Her family and friends were no good. Her job, which she was forced to quit, was stupid. She was stupid. Anything that went wrong in A.H.'s life was blamed on Tippi. And, something was always "wrong." One night, claiming he was "just pissed off" and threatening to kill the entire family, which now included a child, A.H. drove 110 mph up Route 29 from Trenton towards Lambertville.

Any reaction, comment, or protest from Tippi during these attacks led to a beating; and, A.H. made sure she reacted. Over the years, Tippi was repeatedly strangled, kicked, and punched. She was kicked in the face with cowboy boots and choked. In one of the worst beatings, A.H. pushed Tippi to the floor, beating and strangling her to unconsciousness, leaving her hemorrhaging on the floor. The physical abuse was so bad that Tippi miscarried two babies as a direct result of the beatings.

The violence escalated when A.H. quit work and started drinking. That was when he started abusing his son as well. Tippi and her son fled, with police protection, after six years of abuse. That was the only time the police had been called. A.H. moved his girlfriend into the house the following day. (Kramer, Victim, 1998)

*   *   *

Lynn, who is also living in Lambertville, met Matt at the office where they both worked. Matt, labeled the "most eligible bachelor in the corporation," quickly fell for Lynn. The couple married a year later.

There were a few signs of the abuse that was to come before the wedding, such as unexplained absences. But, Matt justified them, telling Lynn he was working a second job.

Over the next few years, Matt successfully built a wall between his real activities and his wife. He always cashed Lynn's paychecks, telling her they were saving for a house. Matt was always saving-to the point that Lynn didn't have enough money for her basic needs. She was given twenty dollars a week for groceries and she was forced to make her own clothes. There was no money to replace Lynn's car when it broke down, leaving her dependent on Matt for transportation during the rare times he wasn't working, and, he insisted on calling her Linda, which was not her name.

When a child arrived, Lynn became more isolated. She had to take a leave of absence from her job to take care of the baby. Matt eventually convinced her to quit her job altogether in favor of being a good mother. With Lynn now totally isolated from friends and family, Matt became more secretive. He started coming home late, claiming he was working late in the office. He demanded dinner be ready when he walked in the door. He would criticize Lynn's cooking, throw her food in the garbage, and storm out to buy take-out. Then, he started coming home after he had eaten, throwing Lynn's dinner in the garbage claiming he wasn't hungry. He criticized her housekeeping, hairstyle, clothing, and family.

The unexplained absences and abusive behavior continued. Matt would leave for his weekend job and not return home until the following day. During vacations, he would disappear for days at a time. He always had an excuse-the car broke down stranding him, he was so tired he pulled over to the side of the road and fell asleep, or he went out with his friends and forgot to call.

Matt was doing none of these things. He was a gambler. Sometimes, the poker games would go on for days. At other times, it was the racetrack that kept him away. He bet on all sporting events at every opportunity, losing thousands of dollars to his bookie.

Lynn meanwhile, was scrubbing bathrooms and waxing the kitchen floor daily in an effort to please her husband. With no money for Christmas presents for her child, she was forced to take a job every holiday season, relying on Matt for transportation. Her jobs were criticized.

Matt would give Lynn money for Christmas and then refuse to give her food money, forcing her to spend her "gift" on family necessities. He would promise to take her out to dinner. Many times she and a baby-sitter were left waiting-because he never came home. She was called names, degraded, and humiliated in public and in private. Then, Matt accused her of seeing a boyfriend every time she went grocery shopping. The accusations and abuse got worse.

Lynn felt trapped and not in control of any aspect of her life. She was being told how to dress, where she could go, and what she should do each day. The dreamed of house had materialized, but there was little furniture. Lynn had to keep her child's clothes in cardboard boxes.

Matt, on the other hand, was foot-loose and fancy-free, coming and going as he pleased, taking no responsibility around the house, and making Lynn's life miserable. When Lynn could take no more abuse, she took her child and left. She was never hit and never called the police. (Kramer, Victim, 1998)

*   *   *

Suzi also escaped the abuse of her estranged husband, Bill, a college graduate, and a heroin addict. Her story is different, with much of the abuse she endured going hand-in-hand with her husband's heroin addiction.

"It started off four years ago before we were married," she said. "I didn't understand, didn't know about heroin and what it does. I caught him using heroin and told him not to use it again or we weren't going to get married, and he said, 'OK.'"

Bill's heroin addiction, as Suzi found out, was only the tip of the iceberg.

"About six weeks after we got married," she continued, "I found $2,000 missing from my savings account. It was like a $300 with-drawal one week and more the next. I confronted him again and asked him where the money went. He denied knowing anything about it and started playing mind games with me, like I paid the bills and did this or that, and that's where the money went.

"He tried to make me think I was stupid," she said. "I realized he was lying and confronted him again. I believed him when he said he wouldn't do it again."

Despite Bill's promises, he continued to use heroin and his abuse worsened.

"I found out that he was still on heroin and I got to know 'the look,'" Suzi said. "He had real pale skin, dark circles under his eyes and pinprick pupils. He was really groggy. He was just a mess with bad acne and stuff.

"I'd confront Bill, and he'd deny he was using heroin, but then I'd wake up in the middle of the night, and he'd be gone," she continued. "He'd say he went out for gas or have another lame excuse. Or I'd get in the shower, and when I'd get out, he'd be gone and stay away for five or six hours.

"He'd come back bleeding with stab wounds or beaten up. He came back with stab wounds in the chest twice," Suzi recalled. "He'd let strange people get in the car, people he was going to buy heroin from, and they tried to rob him and steal the car, and they stabbed him. He was beat up several times. Once, he owed his dealer money, and when he couldn't pay, they beat him up, and his face was all black and blue."

In an effort to keep her marriage together, Suzi supported Bill in his effort to stop using drugs, but she paid a high emotional price.

"Bill was always the worst right before he went into rehab," she said. "It was like he just had to get one more fix. He's been in rehab seven times in the four years we were together."

One time in particular stands out in Suzi's mind. Bill, who was supposed to go into a rehabilitation program in the morning, stole Suzi's car and drove out in a snowstorm in the search of "one more fix." And, as he'd done several times in the past, Bill wound up in an accident, crashing Suzi's car into a Jersey barrier in the blinding snow.

"He crashed all our cars while he was on heroin," she said. "One time, a couple of years ago, when we had that big snow-storm, he stole my car. He was supposed to go into rehab in the morning," she continued, "and we'd taken all his car keys from him, and my brother-in-law was staying with us to try and keep him under control. He actually had to wrestle Bill to the ground. Bill managed to sneak out anyway and somehow got into my car and crashed it into a concrete barrier while he was going to get his heroin. I don't even remember how he got home that night.

"Another time," she said, "I was at the movies with my girl-friend, and when I came out, my car was gone. I finally found it, and it smelled really awful, like beer and other stuff, so I con-fronted Bill. At first, he said he'd been in his Narcotics Anony-mous meeting, but what he'd done was walk two miles to the theater and then stole my car to go get heroin.

"Another time, I was getting my eyes checked, and when I

came out, my car had been broken into, and all my things had been stolen. I found Bill at home, sitting on the floor with all my things spread out around him, going through all my stuff looking for money."

Bill managed to keep Suzi emotionally off balance during their entire relationship.

"Bill was always lying," she said. "After all his promises and lies, I get a call from the police to come pick him up because he fell asleep from heroin and crashed the car. I was nine months pregnant.

"After I had the baby, and I was still in the hospital," Suzi continued, "he disappeared for two days. He crashed the car again then from the heroin.

"After that, he'd sneak out at night to get his heroin or while I was at work so I wouldn't find out. One time, I found him passed out on the floor with five empty heroin bags scattered around in a bunch of garbage. Other times, he'd be jittery or on the floor shaking from withdrawal. One time, he was even foaming at the mouth."

Then, Suzi found out that Bill was doing more than just using heroin, cleaning out her bank accounts, and wrecking their cars.

"I found out that he was stealing prescriptions from our friends and family," she said. "He stole all my father's prescriptions and went through my aunt's cabinets and stole all her medicine, like Tylenol with codeine. Everywhere we went, he stole. He always said he was looking for change for gas money."

As Bill continued to use heroin and steal money and drugs from friends and family, Suzi became more isolated. While she found out about many of these things after she left Bill, what finally prompted her to give up on rehabilitation and leave Bill was the way he interacted with their infant daughter.

She said, "He'd just lay her down on a table and walk away."

But, even after leaving Bill, Suzi is facing the financial consequences of loving an abusive man. She recently found out that she's being sued by a collection agency.

She left Bill, not knowing that Bill had a gasoline credit card in her name that she thought she had discontinued. What she found out was that Bill was driving to Philadelphia to buy his heroin. He'd stop at a gas station and approach a customer, saying he was in need of cash and offering a full tank of gas on "his" credit card in exchange for $10 or $20. Suzi is responsible for the more than $2,000 Bill charged to her account, and she's trying to find out what other credit cards he has that are in her name, believing he has taken advantage of "cash advances" to support his habit.

* * *

None of these victims, despite serious injuries and ongoing patterns of battery and emotional upheaval, chose to involve the police. Few victims do. Women are six times less likely to report domestic violence to the police than women who are victims of stranger violence. (American Psychological Association, 1996, 10) Men are even less likely to summon help.

Of those men and women who have reported domestic violence incidents to the Lambertville Police Department in 1996, (LPD, 1996) a wide variety of abusive behaviors are noted:

- One Lambertville abuser would repeatedly push his wife and hold her down as he shouted profanities at her.
- Another Lambertville abuser assaulted his victim. When she tried to break off their relationship, he vandalized her car.
- One Lambertville batterer kicked and punched his victim in the stomach.
- Others punched and slapped their victims in the face.
- One Lambertville abuser bit and kicked his victim.
- One Lambertville abuser stalked his victim.
- Lambertville abusers threw object such as fans and furniture through windows during assaults.
- One Lambertville man stole his victim's pocketbook after a domestic argument.

- After breaking off their relationship, two Lambertville men engaged in a fist fight.
- Several victims reported their abusers were making threatening phone calls.
- In three of the reported domestic violence incidents, females were the aggressor.

CHAPTER 4

A domestic violence call is the most dangerous situation a police officer can respond to. It is so dangerous that New Jersey guidelines and police training recommend that more than one officer respond to a call of this type.

Of the 55 law enforcement officers feloniously killed during 1996, 21 of them were on duty alone. Eleven others, while working alone, were not the only ones on duty at the time. Seven were on special assignments and seven were off duty. (U.S. Department of Justice/ Federal Bureau of Investigation, 21, 1996) During that same year, a total of 47,251 law enforcement officers were assaulted in the line of duty. (U.S. Department of Justice/ Federal Bureau of Investigation, 65 & 75, 1996) In the ten-year period from 1987-1996, seven of the 696 law enforcement officers who died nationally were from New Jersey (USDOJ/FBI, 23, 1996)

Part of the danger lies within the dispatch system when the victim, a relative, or a neighbor picks up the phone and calls 9-1-1. The person receiving the call for a domestic violence/assault situation in progress may not ask, or the caller may not know, whether any weapons are involved, whether the abuser is still in the house or at the scene, where exactly the abuser is in relation to the scene, the layout of the house or area where the assault is occurring, where exactly the victim is and, if the victim able to escape. These are critical questions for the safety of the victim and the responding officers.

Lambertville Patrolman William McLaughlin describes what it's like to respond to a domestic violence call. (Kramer, Expert, 1998)

"Once you get on scene, the first thing you do is visually survey the outside of the house," he said. "Look at the layout from the outside. Listen for any sounds that might tell you where the assault is taking place and what might be happening. With a violent assault in progress, you have to think about what actions you are going to take to protect not only the victim but also the responding officers. And then, you have to make critical decisions without knowing exactly who is where, or what is happening. And sometimes, you don't know if there are weapons involved.

"Then, we have to determine who is the victim and who is the offender and separate the two," he continued. "The main objective is then to get the offender away from the immediate scene in order to protect the others in the area. Then, we have to figure out what exactly happened. Very often, the serious actions are over by the time we get there and what we find is a lot of confusion, with persons bleeding, victims with red marks on their necks from attempted stranglings, destroyed furniture, yelling and screaming. Our objective then becomes to sort things out and resolve this situation to the point that we don't have to come back again."

Despite the State guidelines recommending that two or more officers respond to a domestic violence call, it is a sad fact that in many communities, there may only be one officer on duty at any given time. And, as Ptl. McLaughlin points out, "Any domestic violence call, from simple harassment to attempted murder, can escalate into a volatile situation within seconds."

For the police officers who are responding to the domestic violence call, they may find themselves the unwilling victims in a twist of misplaced aggression.

"Our arrival is the most dangerous time because people are stressed over what has just happened and emotions are high," Ptl. McLaughlin explained. "This is the time another family member, or the victims themselves, can become the aggressor, turning on the police."

He went on to describe just such a case that he responded to recently.

"We had a case not too long ago in Lambertville, where two

officers responded to a domestic violence call," he said. "As they were trying to cuff the offender, who was struggling on the couch, his two preteen children attacked the officers. The two officers suddenly found themselves wrestling with one adult offender who was trying to escape, and two children who were attacking. The two children even tried to take the officers' guns out of their holsters, and did manage to get one nightstick. One officer was bitten, while the other was kicked and scratched.

"Imagine," he said, "being the only one on duty and having to respond to something like this. One of the biggest obstacles a solitary officer on duty faces when responding to a serious domestic violence call, is making an instant decision about what action to take without putting himself in jeopardy."

Ptl. McLaughlin goes on to say that in Lambertville, where there may only be one officer on duty, the domestic violence problem is so prevalent that you "can almost predict one domestic violence call per night."

The danger to a police officer working alone is best illustrated through the tragic death of an Anchorage, Alaska policeman on October 26, 1996. The officer, a ten year veteran responding to an 11:30 a.m. 9-1-1 domestic disturbance call, recognized the suspect as a man who had an outstanding warrant and a restraining order against him for domestic violence. Wearing body armor, the officer pursued the suspect into a residence.

The suspect, when confronted, shot the officer in the head with a .44 caliber revolver. By the time a backup officer arrived, the first officer, who had now become a victim, was dead. The suspect, meanwhile, went to a neighboring house where he shot and killed a four-year-old boy, a six-year-old girl, and his former wife before turning the gun on himself. (USDOJ/FBI, 41, 1996)

Responding to a domestic violence call not only takes lives and causes injuries, but it takes time; and it can leave a small community vulnerable to other types of crime while the officers are tied up on the domestic violence call.

According to Ptl. McLaughlin, a domestic violence arrest can take an officer off the road for 4-8 hours. If juveniles are involved, he said, it takes even longer. The parties involved in the domestic dispute have to be transported to police headquarters in separate vehicles unless one goes to the hospital, in which case an officer still must accompany that person. At headquarters, both parties must be separated.

"Our policy dictates that these two must not be in same room," Ptl. McLaughlin explained. "When a juvenile is involved, they can not be held in the same room as an adult unless it is with the parent who is the victim. And, an officer must be with the parties involved at all times.

"We have to take statements from everyone and photograph any injuries," he continued. "One officer processes the offender for arrest-fingerprints, photograph, typing warrants, and contacting a judge. The processing for the offender takes 2-4 hours depending on the number of complaints and exactly what happened. The same officer will have to take the offender to jail. According to our domestic violence guidelines, every step of the process must be adhered to-no short cuts."

Ptl. McLaughlin added that, in New Jersey, the police can make probable cause arrests in domestic violence cases when someone has been injured. If no one is injured during the domestic dispute, only the victim and offender have the right to sign complaints against each other. Restraining orders involve 1-2 hours of taking information, filling out forms, and transferring the information to a judge. If the victim is not able or willing to give a statement, or the offender refuses to talk, it can take much longer.

Whether working alone or in pairs, phone calls must be made as soon as possible; off-duty officers must be called in to handle other emergency calls during the processing. Until this officer comes in, Lambertville, like other smaller communities, must rely on neighboring towns to cover calls. Other calls to Victim Advocacy, the Women's Crisis Center, clergy if requested, and/or another family member must also be made. The welfare of the victim is the main concern at this point. One officer will spend his or her entire time with the victim until all notifications and all referrals have been made.

The other officer must now take the offender to jail, which in a simple case, takes about an hour, but it isn't without its dangers. If the offender has been drinking, he can kick back windows out of the police car, launch assaults on the officer with his feet, head, fists, or teeth, or cause other problems.

And, if the abuser is highly drunk, he or she must be deemed medically fit to go to jail, which means a trip to the hospital. The officer must remain with the offender until the emergency room staff judges him sober enough to be medically evaluated. And, other problems can arise.

One Lambertville offender, who was strapped down on a gurney, got out of the restraints, and took off through the emergency room. Another agency had to be called in for backup in capturing the offender. Some officers have had to remain at the hospital a full shift, only to be replaced by an incoming officer from the next shift.

"The arresting agency," Ptl. McLaughlin notes, "is responsible for the offender until custody is turned over to the jail.

"The most frustrating part of a domestic violence call comes when it is time to sort everything out and put it down on paper for the report," he continued. "It becomes more frustrating and annoying with repeats because each time can be a different scenario and the offender is usually bailed out the next day."

While not all domestic violence calls are chaotic and laced with violence, many are.

On November 28, 1996, McLaughlin and fellow patrolman Robert Brown responded to a North Main Street residence for a report of domestic violence with the possibility of a gun being involved. When they arrived at the scene, they found a 37 year old male and his female intimate engaged in a verbal dispute in the front yard, with the abuser holding a shot gun.

As the officers approached the abuser and took the gun away

from him, a large crowd of onlookers gathered, totally blocking traffic on the street.

To further complicate matters, when Ptl. Brown placed the abuser under arrest, he was attacked from behind and hit by a 21-year-old male relative of the abuser, knocking both Ptl. Brown and the abuser to the ground. The abuser then tried to hit Ptl. Brown to avoid being handcuffed as the relative tried to choke him from behind.

Ptl. McLaughlin used pepper spray to subdue the relative and placed him under arrest.

The abuser, who had been successfully handcuffed and was still on the ground, was by this time, kicking and punching both officers as they tried to take him to the waiting police car.

The abuser's sister then got into the act, trying to free her brother by placing herself between him and Ptl. Brown. She kept up her assault, shouting obscenities at the officers as her brother, who had gone limp, was being carried by both officers.

As he was being placed in the patrol car, the abuser's sister turned her attention to the other male relative, attempting to free him from the locked back seat of the other patrol unit.

All three were arrested and charged with a variety of offenses, including aggravated assault on a uniformed police officer.

Interestingly, the offender had been arrested the previous evening for a domestic violence incident at the same location-in which a verbal dispute had escalated to furniture being thrown through a window. He had been released after someone posted bail. (Department Case #96-3362)

CHAPTER 5

Who are these offenders who, because of their own behavior, cause untold suffering to their victims, assault and kill police officers, and take up so much time in the law enforcement and judicial systems?

What kind of a person batters?

For years we have read articles about spousal abuse and battery and have seen people in violent relationships on television shows like "Oprah" and "Sally." The bottom line in these cases is the need for therapy and marriage counseling. Therapy for the batterer, so they can learn to redirect their anger, learn self-control, and stop the abuse. Counseling for the couple, if they want to remain together, so they can mend their broken relationship and learn to deal with their problems in nonviolent ways. Help for the victim, so they realize their own self worth and realize they did not deserve to be battered.

Is battery really a problem of social adjustment, a condition that is treatable, or is it something entirely different?

Some people batter and abuse from the beginning of a relationship. They may have grown up in an abusive home, they may have poor behavior controls, or they simply may not realize their behavior is abusive. The signs of abusiveness may be as subtle as a shove, slap, or a comment. As said previously, the signs of abuse can start during the "dating stage" of the relationship. Some of these batterers can be helped and some can't. The best advice anyone can give the victims in these relationships is, get out. End the relationship immediately.

But, there is another type of abuser. This abuser is wonderful at the beginning of the relationship. He or she is perfect in every

way: intelligent, funny, outgoing, and in all probability, good looking. These are the dangerous ones. They slowly manipulate their
partner, tightening the reins of control and increasing their abuse
until their victim has been unknowingly sucked into a life of domestic violence, under the complete control of their abuser. Let's
take a look at "Stanley." (Cleckley pp176-187)

Stanley was from a good home. He was a college graduate with
a high I.Q. who was successful, not only in school and business,
but in impressing and attracting other people. On the surface, he
was a considerate, handsome, intelligent, confident, hard working
young man who showed great leadership qualities.

But, to those who knew him well, Stanley presented an entirely different picture. Married for the first time while still in
college, Stanley made outrageous demands on his wife, frequently
beating her severely with little provocation. When she would try
to escape the violence, Stanley would lock the doors and hold her
captive. When neighbors called the police, Stanley brushed these
episodes off as being "typically feminine" and "a somewhat ridiculous exaggeration of some minor disagreement."

At the most, he admitted to having taken "mild physical measures to influence her," adding that her habit of screaming and
crying made him lose his temper.

He never acknowledged that the only time she screamed or
cried was during a beating.

Underneath his public face of being a "normal" person, and
despite the likable outgoing nature he presented in public, the
real Stanley was a master con-artist who had multiple marriages,
assumed huge debts, bounced from job to job, cheated on his
wives with numerous affairs, wrote bad checks, ran up massive
phone bills, lied and fabricated stories, and otherwise lived a life
full of illegal and irresponsible behavior. And, he was a batterer.

If we take a close look at the behaviors of the abusers in our
case examples, we can identify and isolate specific battery behaviors and patterns.

As an example, we can say that A.H. demanded that his wife

have dinner ready for him at exactly midnight every night. That is a blanket statement that doesn't really tell us what specific behaviors A. H. displays during these episodes.

If we look at his demands from a behavioral standpoint however, we can see that A. H. goes into a rage if dinner isn't waiting for him and hits, punches, and kicks Tippi into unconsciousness. If his dinner is waiting for him, he measures Tippi's portions and never allows her a second helping. We've now established a pattern of abuse based on A.H.'s behaviors.

From the analysis of the specific behaviors and patterns we have identified, we can now gain some dramatic insights into the characteristics, emotions, motives, and intent of abusers.

For example, it is clear, as demonstrated by A.H.'s daily dinner behavior, that Tippi is going to become the target of her husband's abuse no matter what she does. If dinner isn't ready, she gets beaten. If it is ready, he won't allow her to eat.

One has to wonder if A. H. planned these attacks with the specific intent of controlling, hurting, and humiliating Tippi?

John Douglas, a retired F.B.I. profiler and former head of the F.B.I.'s Investigative Support Unit says, "Behavior reflects personality." (Obsession, 230)

In other words, the way a person behaves, what they do and how they do it-or what they don't do in a given situation-is a reflection of their true self. The specific behaviors of abusers then become evidence that can be analyzed much as a parent would analyze the unacceptable behavior of a child.

To take it a step further, if the generally accepted common characteristics of the victims and the interpretable general information about the locations where the abusive behaviors have taken place are factored in, one can then come to logical conclusions about the specific personality traits, characteristics, and motivations of abusers.

It becomes clear almost immediately that the abuser has no sympathy for his victim. Sympathy is compassion. It is feeling or expressing pity or sorrow for another's distress. Sympathy is the capacity for sharing the feelings of another person.

Would a person who feels sympathy beat a person unconscious and then just walk away, leaving them bleeding on the floor? Or choke someone into unconsciousness as a means of control? Or throw their victim's dinner in the garbage, refusing to eat it?

If the abuser doesn't have sympathy for his or her victim, what then do they have? What the abuser does have is empathy for his victim.

Empathy is understanding someone else's feelings or situation-and, the abuser understands. He knows exactly what he is doing to his victim. He knows he is causing physical or mental pain every time he lashes out.

He knows just how to hit and exactly what to say to cause the pain. He knows what part of the victim's stomach to kick to cause the most suffering, and where his victim's emotional vulnerabilities lie.

But, he doesn't care because he has no sympathy for his victim. He has no feelings about the pain and injury he has just caused. If he did, he would never abuse again.

A lack of remorse is another common characteristic shared by abusers.

"I'm sorry. I love you. It won't happen again." How many times have victims heard these empty words? The abuser talks about "it" as though the abuse was nothing more than a minor discussion. The abuser who left his wife battered and hemorrhaging on the floor simply didn't care that he had inflicted those injuries. If he had, he would have gotten her medical help and never touched her again.

Stanley, our first example shows no remorse when talking about the abuse he inflicted on his wife. He brushed these episodes off as being "typically feminine" and "a somewhat ridiculous exaggeration of some minor disagreement." At the most, he admitted to having taken "mild physical measures to influence her," adding that her habit of screaming and crying made him lose his temper.

He never acknowledged that the only time she screamed or cried was during a beating. As we said, a lack of remorse is a common trait among batterers.

The abuser, whose wife has just left him, rarely makes an honest attempt at changing his behavior. When she leaves, all he thinks about is himself. He never thinks about the weeks, months, or years of humiliation and pain he has put his victim through.

Rather than changing his ways or acknowledging that he and only he was responsible for his behavior and the abuse, the abuser prefers to live with his distorted perception of reality, blaming his wife for screwing up his life. He has no sympathy for his wife and shows no remorse for his actions.

As another example, we saw that A. H. always blamed Tippi when anything went wrong. A. H. was able to parlay that belief into abuse, in fact punishing her for something that he did.

This distorted perception of events is reality in the mind of the abuser. He truly believes it's all the victims fault, so there is nothing for him to be sorry for. (Douglas, Obsession. 279)

The abuser's belief that he's done nothing wrong plays a large part in his lack of remorse. He explains away, minimizes, denies the effects of his behavior, and puts the blame on others; and all the time, in his mind, he believes he's done nothing wrong. And, if he's done nothing wrong, then, there is nothing to be sorry for. (Hare, 1993)

Is domestic abuse and violence something that just happens then, in response to a specific situation? Is it just the result of a "personality flaw" in the abuser? Is the victim in some way responsible?

The answer is a resounding "No" to all of these questions. The behavior of batterers clearly shows that they wait for specific planned opportunities to inflict injury.

Let's take a look at the abusers in our case examples. They were all able to go to work every day and get along with their coworkers and supervisors without any violence. They were able to socialize without violence.

In fact, they all concealed their abusive and violent behaviors well enough in public that they were able to fool the people they came in contact with during their daily activities. These men were able to hold their anger and abusive behaviors in check until they were home.

Brent E. Turvey, a nationally recognized criminal profiler who specializes in behavioral evidence analysis and crime scene reconstruction, agrees.

"The batterers who have a lot to lose must maintain a superficial veneer of personality at work and with friends," he said. "Then they let it out at moments that they are certain they can control (witnesses and environment) and inflict injuries that either cannot be seen or can be explained." (Turvey, Personal, 1998)

When we look at abusive and violent behaviors other than battery, we can see the same indications of planning.

In the case example of Matt and Lynn, we can see how Matt planned his timing when he got home just in time for Lynn to go to the hospital. He always showed up, but he was always just late enough to upset Lynn. And, all the times he promised to take her out and didn't come home? He knew she was waiting for him-because he was the one who had asked her out. He planned his abuse, inviting her out knowing full and well that it would inflict emotional pain when he didn't show up.

It's hard to imagine abusers preparing for their assaults in this way, but they do. They pick safe locations for their assaults-places that will lessen their chances of getting caught by outsiders. They buy bindings and ropes. They take precautionary measures such as disconnecting phones and isolating the victims from family and friends. They bring weapons into the house.

With each kick, punch, or slap, they're learning in preparation for their next attack. When they get "pissed off" at work they hold their anger in. They think about what they are going to do to their victim when they get home. They are making plans and getting ready for their next assault.

And, they take precautionary measures that factor into the abuse scenario.

Precautionary acts, in this case, are purposeful things the batterer does to prevent others from finding out about the abuse. They lower the risks he must take when he abuses. His risks are high; he stands to lose his job, his victim, his children, his position in the community, the respect of his friends and his home. Additionally, if he's caught, he stands a very good chance of spending time in jail. So each and every time he batters, he must make sure that he not only isn't caught, but that his victim won't tell.

Things such as blocking the doorway, locking the doors to prevent escape, hitting or kicking the body where the injuries won't show, and denying medical treatment to prevent authorities from finding out are some ways offenders lower their risk. Other precautionary measures include keeping the blinds or curtains closed so the neighbors can't see in, disconnecting the phones so the victim can't call for help, threatening to kill the victim to insure silence, forcing the victim to quit their job so coworkers won't find out, and isolating the victim from all friends and family so they won't find out.

The selection of the location for the assault is also a precautionary measure. He needs to control the location so the assault will work in his favor. The offender knows he would be putting himself at a great deal of risk if he routinely battered his spouse in the middle of the street, so he chooses a location that will suit his purpose of secrecy and give him the most control over the situation-usually, the home.

He can go one step further if he batters his wife in a room near the children. He knows she's not going to scream or challenge him, putting herself in greater danger, if the children are there, because she will do almost anything to protect them from witnessing the violence or becoming victims themselves.

So many times, we hear of victims falling into glass doors, down a flight of steps, or having some other type of "accident." Abuse and battery aren't inflicted by accident or mistake. One person doesn't strangle another or destroy their possessions by mistake. Alex didn't sexually abuse his children by mistake. A. H. didn't drive up Route 29 at 110 mph by accident. Burning someone with a lit cigarette or killing their pets aren't accidents. These are all purposeful actions.

Abuse isn't triggered by stress, drugs, or alcohol, either. Many victims blame their abuser's behavior on alcohol or drug use, trying to rationalize that it is the influence of the drugs or alcohol that causes the behavior. They think if he stops drinking or taking drugs, the beatings will stop. One simple question provides the answer: Is he randomly beating up people on the street or at work? No, because domestic abuse and violence are purposeful behaviors. (Metro, 1998)

CHAPTER 6

The abuser knows what he is doing with each specific act of abuse he commits. He has learned through repeated assaults just what he has to do to inflict the damage he intends. Maybe he shoved the first time. Shoving didn't get the result he wanted, so he hit the second time. Did he hit his victim in the face? Did it leave marks? Maybe the next time he punched his victim in the stomach where the injuries wouldn't show. The abuser demonstrates his knowledge of what he's doing every time he lands a punch or makes a derogatory comment.

Just as abusers plan out their assaults, they become masters of control and use many different methods to maintain a tight hold on their victims and isolate them from anyone who could help them escape the abuse. They kick, choke, and intimidate in their efforts to control.

Simply getting the victim to respond, no matter how negatively, is, in the mind of the abuser, a sign that he has control because he has gotten her to do what he wants her to do. One example of this would be the husband who constantly belittles his wife for wearing makeup. When she finally stops using cosmetics, he has scored a victory. He has gotten her to do exactly what he wanted her to do; he has gained control over another aspect of her life and has chiseled away one more piece of her identity.

The battered wife, cowering and bleeding in the corner of the kitchen feeds into the ego of the abuser. He sees her behavior as the proof of his ability to control. The abuser is effectively getting what he wants through control by instilling fear and submission in his victim.

Many of the precautionary acts taken by abusers are also means of control. Beating his wife up in the kitchen of his home, while affording the offender the safety of privacy, is also a control, because his victim is suffering the assault in a location that affords her no escape. Gags to prevent screaming, and bindings to prevent escape are also methods of control.

Another form of control is control of the situation. The abuser is careful to choose a location for the battery that will give him total control over the situation and that location is almost always his home. Think about this: How many victims of domestic violence do we see getting beaten up in public?

If we look at the case of Sally and Alex, the concepts become clear. Alex wanted to sexually abuse his children. Alex's precautionary acts included the choice of location and timing of the sexual assaults on his children. He couldn't sexually abuse them in the middle of the street, in the park, or at a movie. He made sure the abuses occurred in the house, which was a safe place to perform that type of activity, with little risk of him being found out. He also knew that he couldn't sexually abuse his children with Sally in the house. So, he took another precautionary act and got rid of her.

He purposely chose Sunday nights, making sure Sally wouldn't come home by allowing her to do something she wanted to do.

Alex then had to take more precautionary measures with the children to further lower his risk. He had to gain the confidence of the children and convince them that what he was about to do to them was all right. He had to make sure that he didn't leave any suspicious marks on the children as a result of the abuse. And finally, Alex had to assert enough control over them to make sure they wouldn't tell about the abuse. Intimidation tactics and threats worked.

How many times did he think about the children and Sunday night during the week? He knew exactly what he was doing and it wasn't a mistake or accident when he performed the actual abuses.

When he was finally caught, Alex gave a glib answer. He shrugged the years of abuse off as something inconsequential because he didn't care that he had inflicted a lifetime's worth of emotional damage on his children. He had no remorse for what he did and displayed no sympathy for the plight of his children. Many abusers develop high levels of skill in their efforts to control and dominate. Abusers know that to be successful, they have to keep their victim emotionally off balance. They will be loving one moment and violent the next. They will attempt to control every aspect of the victim's life, always pulling the reins in a little tighter. They play mind games, check the mileage on the car, and monitor phone calls. With each incident, the abuser is practicing and developing his skills of abuse, learning what to do and how to do it most effectively.

He learns to hit without leaving marks. He learns how to abuse sexually without getting caught. He learns how to choke his victim, letting go just before or as she loses consciousness.

Many of these behaviors, such as monitoring everyday activities, checking mileage, and counting money are also stalking and surveillance activities that become part of the abuser's routine and become useful to the offender when the victim leaves. (Douglas et al Obsession 270)

In our fourth case example, Matt demonstrates his skill levels at keeping Lynn emotionally off balance by promising to take her out to dinner and then not showing up. Another of his "mind games" surrounded Lynn's desire to volunteer at a hospital. After making it clear that he thought it a stupid waste of her time, he finally consented. Lynn in turn, always checked with Matt before she committed herself to a specific time. She made sure that there was no conflict with his schedule because she was dependent on his car for transportation.

What did Matt do? He pulled in the driveway at the exact time Lynn was supposed to be starting her volunteer work, causing her a great deal of anxiety wondering if he was actually going to show up. Then, she had the worry and embarrassment of being late every time. (Kramer, Victim, 1998)

Other abusers use the skills they have learned elsewhere when they assault. Does he enjoy boating or sailing? What types of rope and/or knots does he use in his abuse? Chances are, he uses the same ones that he uses on his boat.

Was he in the military? Was he trained in hand-to-hand combat or the martial arts? How does he hit? Where does he hit? The chances are he has learned to adapt his martial arts skills to use them as part of the batteries.

Was he trained in the use of weapons? What weapons does he use in his assaults? How does he handle those weapons? Again, the chances are that he uses the weapons he's familiar with, and he uses them to his advantage during the assaults.

Weapons can mean knives, guns, ropes, straps for binding, belts for beating, electrical prods, or anything else that can be used to inflict threats, control, or injury. In New Jersey, 3,332 people were seriously injured by weapons during domestic violence incidents in 1996. Of those, 191 were shot and 863 were stabbed or slashed by knives. Other types of weapons such as bats, clubs, pipes, ropes, etc. were the cause of 735 additional serious injuries to domestic violence victims. (NJSP, 1996, 195) One must ask if the abuser keeps weapons in the house? If so, why? Are they there because he's an avid hunter or a collector of antique weapons? Or, are they just used during the assaults?

All of these behavioral factors: lack of sympathy, lack of remorse, planning, preparation, precautionary acts, knowledge, lack of mistake or accident, skill, and control come together with each assault, be it an attempted murder or a carefully placed comment. They form the backbone of the individual abuses and take the form of M.O., signature aspect, and ritual, and together, can tell us why the abuse is happening. Then, we will be able to take a look at the fantasy, the power source for the machine known as domestic violence.

CHAPTER 7

M.O. (Modus Operandi), or method of operating, is what the abuser has to do to get what he wants. As an example, if someone wanted to rob a bank, he would in all probability need a disguise such as a mask, a ski cap, or bandanna to avoid being identified, gloves to avoid leaving fingerprints, something to carry the money in, a weapon or some other means of control, and a means of escape such as a car.

He would also have to give thought as to what would be the best day of the week and time of day to pull the heist; he wants to optimize the amount of cash he gets while taking the lowest risk possible. In other words, he doesn't want to enter the bank between 3:00 and 5:00 p.m. on a Friday afternoon when the bank will be full of people cashing their paychecks. Neither does he want to enter the bank just after the vault has been locked for the night. These things are all part of what the robber has to do to successfully rob the bank, and they are his M.O.

Abusers have a method of operating, also. They may use specific locations, bindings, weapons, threats, or violence; anything that he uses or does that he has to use or do to accomplish what he wants forms his M.O.

As an example, let us suppose a female abuser wants to assert more control on her husband who has to take a business trip. Ideally, she'd like to prevent him from going, and at the very least, make sure he has a miserable time. She can take several approaches.

She can sabotage his car by slashing the tires, draining the gas, or disconnecting some hoses-any of these things will cause a major delay in his leaving.

She can threaten to kill his pet, burn his clothes, or destroy his collections while he's gone. Just the thought of these things happening will insure that he has an anxious and miserable time while he's away.

Or, she can slip something into his food to make him sick or hit him in a visible place that leaves cuts and bruises. Then, he'll have to stay home.

No matter what she chooses to do, she must make plans to be sure that her actions are effective. When she makes these plans, she will be planning her M.O.-deciding exactly what she has to do to be effective and not get caught.

If she decides to sabotage the car by slashing the tires, she will need a sturdy knife, a screwdriver, or other object that will cause the damage. She is then going to have to pick a time to slash the tires that will insure that she won't get caught, either by her husband or her neighbors. So, if she decides to sneak out of the house in the middle of the night to do it, she's going to have to wear dark clothes to lessen her chances of being spotted. And, she might even make sure that her husband has a few stiff drinks before bed to make sure he won't wake up and find her gone.

There may be other things that an abuser does while he's on his quest for control. Although they will be part of the battery or assault, these things are not things he or she has to do to; and they are not a necessary part of the abuse. This element of abuse is called signature.

Signature is everything else a person does during the abuse, the extra things that he doesn't have to do, but does anyway. These things could include the use of a specific type of binding, special knots, specific language, ordering the victim to say certain things, biting, pinching, hitting, kicking, doing things in a special order, or any action, thing, or word that is used for domination, manipulation, or control.

These signature behaviors are meaningful to the offender and are based on his or her individual personality.

Let us suppose that our bank robber wore a cartoon character mask and carried a girl's pink purse when he robbed banks. The use of a mask, while being necessary to the committal of the crime, is not unusual; but carrying the pink purse and wearing the cartoon character mask are signature behaviors because they go beyond what is necessary to commit the crime.

The uniqueness of these things that the bank robber feels he must use marks them as signature behaviors and they are the things that may identify him specifically as the offender throughout successive robberies.

Looking at the case example of Bunny and Sam, we can see that Sam planned his late night sexual assaults on Bunny because he waited until Bunny was in a sound sleep and then woke her up, demanding sex rather than going to bed the same time she did. That was Sam's M.O.-waking Bunny up was what he had to do if he wanted to disturb her sleep and force her into sex in the middle of the night.

When Sam went beyond that point and incorporated breaks for alcohol, cigarettes, and crying episodes into what Bunny called their "lovemaking," he introduced signature behaviors. And, the overall signature aspect, which is the emotional or psychological theme the abuser satisfies when he commits the assault, can be deduced from the signature behaviors. (Turvey, CP, 1998)

Sam very simply wanted to accomplish three things with these attacks. First, he wanted to disturb Bunny's sleep. By demanding sex during the middle of the night, he accomplished that. And by disturbing her sleep for hours at a time, he kept her in a constant state of exhaustion. Unlike Sam, Bunny had to get up and go to work in the morning, and it was she who did the house and yard work. She was so tired all the time that she didn't have the energy to challenge Sam or fight back.

Secondly, Sam was using his cigarettes, crying, and drink breaks to keep Bunny on an emotional roller coaster. He would go from a loving, caring, intimate husband into a ranting, crying maniac in a matter of seconds. Then, he'd calmly continue having sex. Then, he'd stop to tell Bunny about how she wasn't his fantasy woman.

Then more sex. Then, Sam would have a drink and a cigarette, add a few tears, and then become the loving husband again.

Thirdly, Sam's overall behavior was meant to degrade and humiliate Bunny. He proved that when he began urinating on the rug and demanding that Bunny clean it up.

If we examine Sam's behaviors from a profiling point of view, we note that his approach was that of surprise, in that he woke Bunny from a sound sleep. He surprised her.

These were carefully planned attacks. By waking Bunny as he did, Sam caught her off-guard at a time when she was groggy and most likely not to resist; he had taken precautionary measures to reduce his risk and insure his success.

Sam was concerned only with himself. He could have accomplished his goals by allowing Bunny to go back to sleep and then waking her up again. He could have taken breaks to talk quietly and intimately with Bunny. He could have taken a shower, or any number of things to interrupt their "lovemaking," but he chose the same scenario over and over again.

He demanded, gave instructions, talked of his sexual fantasies, compared Bunny negatively to his fantasy partner, and used her only as a sexual prop, stopping to have a drink, a cigarette, or to play emotional mind games before resuming his conquest. These were all Sam's signature behaviors.

In this case, Sam's theme, aside from the humiliation he inflicted on Bunny, was total sexual conquest and control.

Sometimes, the signature behavior becomes so important to the abuser that it becomes part of his MO. Let's take the example of an abuser who is stalking his former wife. He routinely leaves threatening notes on the windshield of her car in the middle of the night. He knows that finding the notes in the morning frightens and unsettles her. He knows that she doesn't sleep well because she knows he's going to be there putting the note on the car. That's what he has to do to keep her off balance.

But then, he goes one step further. He leaves a rose with the note, his "statement of his undying love." This is his signature.

And, it represents his fantasy, the perfect relationship that he perceives he has with his victim, a fantasy created in his mind based on his obsession with her. Once he starts leaving the rose with every note, he has then incorporated his signature into his M.O., because it has become part of what he has to do in his nightly routine.

Sam, like the abuser who leaves a rose with the note, incorporated his signature behaviors into his M.O. and his nightly behaviors became part of what he had to do.

Every abuser knows what he has to do to get what he wants. His M.O. may remain consistent, or it may evolve and change as he learns and improves his abusive skills, because M.O. is learned behavior.

An example would be a carjacker attempting to steal his first car. If he goes up to a car and politely asks the driver to get out, the driver will in all probability laugh and drive away. The carjacker will quickly learn that his method of approach isn't going to work. He has to change something in order to be successful.

The next time, the carjacker takes a gun to use as a threat and acts aggressively towards the driver. This time, he gets the car. He has learned what does and doesn't work and has changed his M.O. accordingly.

The abuser learns and changes his M.O. as well, based on his past experiences of what does and doesn't work effectively. His signature behaviors may be subtle, but they will also be there. There may be different signature behaviors with different acts of abuse, but they will always send a message, and they will remain consistent.

Ritual is something the abuser does during an assault that has meaning only to him. A good example of this is Tippi's description of A.H.'s attacks. She describes them as being predictable and methodical. His assaults on her were similar to an actor following a script. A.H. had a ritual that he followed when he beat his wife, and he followed that ritual, doing the same things, in the same order, and in the same way each and every time. When the victim knows what's coming next in the abuse, or in what order he will do things to her, it's a ritual that the abuser, for his own reasons, must follow.

In the same way, Sam's behaviors became ritualistic. Bunny always knew what was going to happen next; and Sam was so wrapped up in his ritual that he even said the exact same things every night when he spoke about his fantasy lover and described the ways he was going to kill himself.

CHAPTER 8

Many of the behaviors displayed by abusers are linked to fantasy, which begins in the mind of the abuser. And, herein lies the heart and soul of domestic violence. The fantasy theme of degradation and control, with the abuser playing the role of "God" and the victim playing the role of "slave," runs rampant in abusive relationships. This theme and the specific behaviors are found from the simplest acts of intimidation to forced sexual acts, nonconsensual sexual bondage, and ritualized beatings.

With the fantasy behaviors firmly in place, the abuser is in full control of the world he has created. The victim is nothing more than the person the abuser has chosen-and needs-not only to make the fantasy come true, but to reinforce the fantasy.

And, the abuser will maintain the fantasy world he has created in the privacy of his home, putting on the facade of superficial normalcy that enables him to work and socialize among his peers without raising suspicions of his true nature.

The victim is in the most danger when reality doesn't live up to the fantasy. (Douglas, Obsession, 226) Remember, the abuser wants to accomplish something when he abuses or assaults his victim. He might tell his victim he wants cooperation, obedience, or sex. But, he doesn't ask nicely or behave in socially accepted ways. He hits, kicks, swears, chokes, yells, and belittles. None of these behaviors are necessary or even productive. In fact, they do a lot more harm than good. And, if the behavior isn't necessary or productive, then what is the real intent behind the assault?

The intent is to reinforce the fantasy, to totally control and dominate another human being by instilling fear, pain, humiliation, and worthlessness onto the victim through signature behaviors.

In the case of the Lambertville batterer who beat his wife and left her hemorrhaging on the kitchen floor, we see an abuser who has inflicted "overkill" type wounds, that is extreme wounds to the face, head, or body that are inflicted through the use of excessive force. He went well beyond what he had to do to get what he wanted.

The abuser who commits this type of attack is nearly identical in typology to the Anger Retaliatory offender. An attack of this nature has its own unique characteristics that are separate from control or dominance motivated attacks and can be broken down into Fantasy Oriented and M.O. Oriented behaviors.

The M.O. Oriented behaviors include the location of the attack and the methods of control used. The Fantasy Oriented behaviors include the victim selection, verbalizations, items used in the attack, any sexual acts and their nature, injuries, amount and type of force used, and the offender's response to any resistance.

The actual attack itself will be a blitz, coming with no warning. The abuser will use angry hostile language, blaming the victim for events or perceived events. The victim will be beaten with anything he can get his hands on and direct excessive force will be used in the battery causing severe injuries.

This type of attack can be so extreme that the victim might be killed. The victim may also be raped as an extension of the attack.

When the attack is directed to the head and face area of the victim, it becomes a direct, personal attack, with the offender taking out his rage for something he perceives the victim did to or against him. This type of attack can occur anytime he gets "pissed off," at any time or any place during the day.

One must wonder, then, if we can narrow domestic violence down to a "cause" that is based in fantasy, can counseling or therapy "cure" the problem?

No. Counseling is a long-term process, not something that will work in a few weeks, or even months. Short-term batterer-intervention programs lasting up to three months have proven to be ineffectual in stopping the battery. While some of the batterers showed an immediate improvement, they reverted to their abuse and violence over time-and, others learned how to abuse and intimidate their victims in a more sophisticated way. (American Psychological Association, Violence, 1996, 11.)

If we think about the behaviors, motivations, and fantasies of the abuser and then factor in the planning and learning that takes place over the course of possibly years of abuse, it is only logical that abusers, when thrown together to talk about the "how and why" of abuse would pick up how-to "tips" on abuse in short-term group counseling sessions. To take this concept one step further, one must realize that all of these abusers have been caught, exposed, and put into counseling because their precautionary and control measures failed. In the abusers mind, it is time to re-think all the things they do when they abuse and batter and come up with some new ways to abuse without getting caught again. And who better to turn to for new ideas than their fellow abusers?

Less than 1% of the known batterers voluntarily seek counseling. The victim will know if the counseling is successful when he has been in counseling for a very long time and he accepts the full responsibility for his violence.

But, beware of the pitfalls. If he says, "I'll go into [or continue] counseling if you come back" or, "You go with me" or, "I've been to counseling, I won't do it any more" or, "I've stopped drinking" or, "I've been going to church every Sunday and I found God," don't believe him. These are nothing more than ploys to regain control of the victim. (MNPD, 1996)

If the victim goes back to the abuser at this stage, the abuse will only begin again, as we will see later in the continuing case of Bunny and Sam. The words the abuser says at this stage are nothing but empty words that the abuser knows the victim wants to hear, and they're designed to lure the victim into a false sense of security for the express purpose of getting her back.

It becomes clear then, that counseling, for the most part, will not work. If anything, it will teach the batterer how to get better at what he does. He will learn new ways to hurt, new precautionary measures to take, and better methods of control. And, the abusive personality doesn't necessarily limit himself to domestic violence.

One must wonder about the abuser. We have seen a person who can lead a "normal" public life while committing sometimes-horrific crimes in the privacy of their homes. Do they really limit their illegal activities to their homes?

Not one of the batterers in our case examples limited their crimes to spousal abuse. One abuser, A.H., had a secret second family-a wife and children. Bill routinely stole items of value and money from friends and family, rifling through desks, drawers, and purses when he'd visit. He also used threats and physical violence to force people to give him money.

Matt was involved in "white collar crime," routinely stealing office supplies. He also ran a stolen goods ring, stealing and then reselling items that his "clients" had ordered. And then, he ran a bookmaking ring.

Sexual abuse of children, adultery, auto theft, and failure to pay creditors were just some of their illegal activities. None of these men were ever arrested for their crimes. Some were able to talk their way out of prosecution. Some of them simply moved, leaving no forwarding address, to avoid prosecution for bad debts and failure to pay child support like Alex did.

As we have seen, the violent and abusive behavior develops from a need to control and dominate. It is a means of boosting the abuser's self-esteem.

The abuser is in fact, living in an illusion; a fantasy of his own creation-not a relationship based on love and caring, but based on the feeling of power he gets from dominating another human be-ing.

It is his way of compensating for being an inadequate person-ality because he is unable to cope with his emotions and lacks self-control.

"When you think about it, if the abuser needs to make his victim even lower than himself, and he's a completely inadequate person, then his victim has to assume a subhuman role. She goes from being wife to property." (Douglas 271)

As we will find out, the abuser who stalks his victim after she has finally left has one objective, and that is to get his victim back in his life. When he finds that he's losing, he may switch his thinking around and decide to go for the ultimate act of control and punishment-murder. (Douglas, Obsession, 281) He will do whatever is necessary to perpetuate the fantasy. It's all part of the circle called love.

CHAPTER 9

Holmes (1996) describes the stages that make up the circle that continually spins throughout the abusive relationship-and he breaks it down into five distinct states-Distorted Thinking, The Fall, Negative Inward Response, Negative Outward Response, and Restoration.

As we have shown, the abuser lives in a fantasy world he has created in his own mind. In this world, the abuser is a competent, well-adjusted individual who has a wonderful job, good friends, an impeccable spouse, and family. Everything runs smoothly, and the abuser, in his or her fantasy, is living the perfect life.

He is living in a psychological state of *distorted thinking* and will remain in this state until something happens to challenge his reality. It might be something real; or, it might be something that he perceives as real in his mind. The abuser might interpret a comment made by a coworker as a personal slight, or an average job review from his boss as a personal attack on his perceived superiority. It can be just one thing or a series of things, but when his reality is challenged, the abuser always takes it personally.

Even though the event that triggers *the fall* may be trivial, the abuser will focus on that event. He will blow it out of proportion and turn it into the most important event in his life; and it will challenge his perfect world and his inflated ego.

Once this happens, the abuser is forced to face the truth of his own inadequacy. This *negative inward response* really sets him off. He starts telling himself that he's too important to be treated that way. Remember, he has a huge ego, and he thinks he's just about the greatest thing on this earth. The psychological conflict that he now finds himself in is the reality of his own inadequacy versus his distorted perception of himself. He's now in a complete tailspin, and the only way he can validate himself or prove his self-worth is to fight back. Mentally, he's thinking, "I don't have to take that from anybody. I'm too important for that."

His *negative outward response* is explosive. He has to prove his superiority and his importance to himself.

Does the abuser confront his boss, coworker, friend, or whoever it is that he holds responsible for the perceived slight? No. He carefully chooses his victim. The abuser needs a victim who is vulnerable because he can't risk another challenge to his reality. The abuser needs a victim that he can control and feel superior to— the one person who will, by becoming his victim, revalidate himself in his own mind. Someone who is, in the abuser's mind, already beneath him and worthless. His intimate. He goes home and beats the crap out of her. And by now, it's all her fault.

After the abuser has proven his superiority to himself, he has reached the stage of *restoration*. It's only now that the abuser starts to think about the potential consequences of his actions. He has put himself at risk. He could lose his job or go to jail. He has to do something above and beyond his precautionary acts to keep his intimate from leaving, telling, or calling the police. This is when the hollow words come into play.

"I'm sorry. I love you. It will never happen again." He will do whatever he feels he has to do to minimize his risk and he'll apologize, cry, send flowers, and make worthless promises.

And, the circle of violence will start all over again, because the abuser, after saying those words, buying flowers, or whatever he does to appease the situation, is once again back in his state of *distorted thinking*.

This cycle continues and repeats itself until the intimate or spouse tries to leave. And, it's at this point, that the victim is in the most danger.

How dangerous are these abusers who view their intimate as an object, nothing more than a prop to be used? Very.

- A research study done at Johns Hopkins University in 1991 showed that murder is the leading cause of death in infants less than one year of age.
- One third of them are victims of abuse or battery.
- The rest died by suffocation, stabbing, gunshot, deliberate drowning, strangulation, and purposeful neglect or abandonment.
- The main reason men give for murdering their intimates is possessiveness-the fear of infidelity, fear of the victim ending the relationship or jealousy over sexual rivalry. (Rasche, 1993)
- Males are four times more likely to use lethal violence than females. (Florida Governor's, 1997, 44, table 7)
- Each year, 3.3 million children are exposed to violence against their mothers or female caretakers. (American Psychological Association, 1996, 11)
- 27% of domestic homicide victims are children. (Florida Governor's, 1997, 51, table 28)
- 90% of the children killed during a domestic dispute are under age 10. 56% are under age 2. (Florida Governor's, 1997, 51, table 28.
- More than 17% of domestic homicide victims had a protection order against their abuser at the time they were killed. (Florida Governor's, 1997, 46, table 15)

All of the authorities on domestic violence agree that the most dangerous period in an abusive relationship is just before or just after the victim has left. During this period of the relationship, the motives and behaviors of the batterer are the same as they were while the couple was together. The batterer, however, on top of being in a total rage, is faced with a new challenge at this stage. His victim isn't waiting for him at home where he can simply walk in the door and beat her up. So, he has to develop new strategies, new ways of getting to her, new methods of approach, and new methods of control. (Douglas, Obsession, "If I Can't Have You, Nobody Will")

It is important to understand that the abuser has just had his entire world yanked out from under him. He's gone through the circle of violence and he's stuck in the *negative inward response* stage. His reality has been shaken to its foundation. He's telling himself that he's been too good of a husband and provider for this treatment. He doesn't have to take this abuse from her. But, the one person he needs, the only person who in his mind is totally worthless, the only one that can be his victim, has just left him.

He's more pissed off than he's ever been in his life.

Rather than facing the reality of his need to control and dominate, his dependency on the relationship, or his own inadequacy as a human being, the abuser puts the blame for his next behaviors squarely on the shoulders of the victim. He rationalizes his need to control his intimate as his obligation or right as a good husband, with the violence dismissed as something caused by the victim-something she did that caused him to react violently. (Douglas, 270)

It is this stage of the violent relationship that all of the abusers inadequacies, personality defects, irrational thinking, fantasies, and reality collide. He has suffered the ultimate rejection because his intimate, the one person in the world he needs to feed and perpetuate his fantasy, has walked out on him.

She has challenged his reality and his perception of life. And, she has asserted herself in the worst way possible, by taking back the reins of control and walking out on him.

He is driven by anger, revenge, and the obsessive need to restore his reality and put himself back in control. In order to do this, he has to get her back, and he will do whatever it takes to accomplish his goal. He may become loving, caring, concerned, and attentive. Or, he may go after her with a vengeance. He becomes a simple-obsession stalker.

Douglas says the abuser will rationalize his stalking behaviors in one of two ways when the victim leaves. He will try to win his victim back by reverting to the charming, loving, attentive person he was at the beginning of the relationship. If that doesn't work, he'll resort to intimidation tactics. Or, he may take a different approach entirely and go after her as punishment for leaving him. (Obsession, 271)

CHAPTER 10

Let's go back to our case examples and take another look at Bunny and Sam.

Bunny started receiving letters and phone calls almost immediately after leaving Sam. Sam, through persistence, flowery displays of emotional regret, and his statements of undying love, was able to convince Bunny to meet with him several weeks later. Let's see how he was able to do that and what happened next:

> Bernadette,
>
> I miss you so terribly my love. I need to see you, to hold you in my arms, to kiss you, and to touch you. You know how deeply I'm in love with you sweetheart. I can not stand not seeing you and not holding you. I know that seeing you will hurt, but I hurt so terribly bad already that I can't imagine it hurting worse than it already does. I love you, my love; I need to be with you. You know that you are the love of my life and that I've never had a love like yours before. Bernadette, I can't lose you my love, I can't lose the greatest love I've ever known. I need so terribly to be with you. I have to stop now, my love, it's very difficult writing this to you. It's just making me so very upset.
>
> I will love you forever,
> Sam

Yes, this is the same Sam who dumped Bunny's food in the garbage, couldn't hold a job, and spent all day on the Internet in search of his fantasy lover. And the same Sam who urinated on the carpeting every night and interrupted his middle of the night sexual attacks for alcohol, cigarettes, and crying rages.

If we look at the letter closely, we can see that nothing has changed. Sam goes on and on about how much he loves Bunny, and yet, he never once shows any interest in her or her feelings. It's all I, I, I. He's still calling her Bernadette. And, it's all Bunny's fault for leaving him.

Although she was cautious, Bunny loved the attention she was getting. Sam wrote daily, professing his love and needs.

He phoned and Bunny took his calls. And, even though she had left him because of his abuse, she felt that she didn't want to be spiteful and she didn't want to hurt Sam.

By giving in and taking his phone calls, Bunny was losing control. Sam had gotten Bunny to do what he wanted her to do.

The calls and letters continued. Three weeks later, the letters changed ever so slightly. While he was still professing his love, Sam was begging Bunny to call him NOW. Meet with him NOW. They had to put the relationship back together, NOW. Sam was making demands and Bunny responded.

She agreed to meet Sam at a local restaurant. They had a wonderful time. Sam drank soda, proof in Bunny's mind that he had quit drinking. He wooed Bunny, and she was responding. Sam was gaining more and more control over Bunny.

They began to date. Bunny thought they should approach their relationship cautiously and refused to see him during the week. At first, they got together just on Saturdays. Then, Saturday and Sunday.

Sam took Bunny out on the Delaware River for a romantic paddlewheel boat ride. He took her on the mule barge. He took her to all the places she had ever wanted to go.

Sam did not touch one drop of alcohol on their dates. He told Bunny he had enrolled in counseling. He said he loved Bunny.

And, he cried-but only when he was completely alone with Bunny. If anyone happened to come upon them, Sam put on a smile and instantly forgot his tears. Bunny rationalized that Sam would have been embarrassed if he were caught crying.

Bunny didn't see Sam's crying as a purposeful behavior aimed at getting her to feel sorry for him. She didn't realize that he was attempting to put the blame for their breakup on her. She didn't see that he was trying to get her to say she was sorry and return home. And, Bunny didn't notice that Sam could turn the tears on and off at will.

The letters kept coming, but then, their tone changed.

> Dear Bernadette,
>
> I know I'm not the man you married, honey, and I don't need to get into specifics right now. The only thing I will guarantee to you is that I will again be that man for you.
>
> Please talk with me honey; there is so much I have held in that now needs to be brought out so that everything can go back to the loving and caring way it used to be.
>
> Please Bernadette, just you and me, let's go away this weekend, so we can get back to the way it was. I love you dearest.
>
> I can fix this nightmare, honey. I just need you by my side. Please let's talk. I do love you very much Bernadette and I will do anything to work this out. It is very important that I speak with you as quickly as possible.
>
> Please call me as soon as possible. I can't stress how important it is that I speak to you. I won't keep you long but there are a few things I need to know now.
>
> Love,
> Sam

This letter was filled with urgency. Sam had so many things to explain. He told Bunny that he knew why he had behaved abusively towards her. He knew, now, why he had been drinking. If they just had one weekend together, he could explain everything.

Bunny weighed her options. For years, she had been begging

Sam to go away for a weekend together. It was tempting, but she wasn't sure if she was ready to take that big of a step. Bunny finally consented to spending one night with Sam-at their house. For Bunny, it was a wonderful, romantic, and loving night. They talked. They made love. And Sam assured her of his undying love.

But Sam was really just tightening the reins and gaining more control. Within three weeks, Bunny had moved back home.

- *The average woman will leave her abuser seven or eight times before making a final break from the circle of violence.* (Standard-Times, 1995)

Two weeks later, Bunny left Sam for good. He had started abusing her, drinking, and urinating on the carpet her second night back.

Sam instantly moved into the next stage of separation. As Douglas explains, after failing in the attempt to win the victim back, the next stage is intimidation, where the abuser becomes increasingly harassing and threatening. (272)

Sam switched tactics, admitting to having made a mistake and begging Bunny's forgiveness. He puts the ultimate blame, however, on Bunny's "fragile" state and then hints at suicide.

> Dear Bernadette,
>
> Please forgive me, I made a terrible mistake. It is a mistake I will never make again. I love you honey and I will never do anything to jeopardize that love again. I felt very comfortable with you here and started an old habit that I shouldn't have; especially after all the weeks that have passed without it.
>
> Forgive me for my indiscretion. I am just totally sick about this situation.
>
> I made a mistake that will never happen again. I did not realize just how fragile you are at this moment. You are the love of my life, sweetheart; please trust me.
>
> I love you.

P.S. I have hurt us both. I screwed up honey, big time. I am in so much pain right now that I don't know what to do. I can't go on without you in my life. I will never screw up again. Please believe me.

Bunny had spent too many nights listening to Sam ranting about the ways he would kill himself not to know what his "P.S." was referring to. But, the memories of the abuse were too fresh in her mind. She ignored his letters and refused his phone calls, all the while holding herself responsible if Sam should kill himself, which is exactly what Sam intended.

The letters continued, each one more abusive than the last. She wrote back to Sam, telling him that she wasn't coming back. Bunny then began to take Sam's calls at work, and she told him she was getting her own apartment.

Bunny was responding to Sam. He still had a chance at regaining full control.

When Bunny moved into her own apartment, she notified her previous landlord that she would no longer be responsible for any rent or other bills incurred by Sam. Sam's writing campaign intensified, putting the blame for his problems squarely on Bunny's shoulders. His hints of suicide became more direct as Bunny refused to have any face-to-face contact with him.

Dear Bernadette,

What are you trying to do to me. Do you care so little about me or hate me so much [that you would tell our landlord lies about me so that he told me to get out of our home immediately.]

Do you want to see me dead; do you hate me that much. We have the greatest love that either of us has ever known and you want to see me destroyed. You know that I love you more than life itself and yet you spit on me like I'm a piece of trash. I'm your husband, Bernadette, the man who loves you very deeply. How can you do this to me. Do you now hate me so much that you want me thrown out of our home. Do you truly want me dead.

. . . Maybe you can explain to me how the man who loves you more than life itself can be tossed aside so easily. . . you must surely enjoy pushing me deeper into this hell I'm in because a considerate person would never do what you've done to me.

Everything I have is yours. I would like Joey to have my collections unless you need to sell them for whatever cash you can get.

If there is a God, I hope he's a forgiving God.

This is all such a waste.

I will love you for eternity.

Your lover and husband,
Sam

This letter reveals a lot about Sam's state of mind at this stage of the separation. He has more than planted the idea that he is going to kill himself if Bunny doesn't return. He has even told her how he wants his possessions divided up after he kills himself, a statement that is meant to reinforce the idea that he is going to commit suicide. He's managed to get the point across that even after she's compelled him to kill himself that he will still love her and he is leaving everything to her as proof.

Sam is doing everything he can to intimidate Bunny and make her feel responsible, guilty, and cruel in her actions towards him. He loves her, but she hates him. He would never hurt her; how could she do this to him? He is accusing her of lying to the landlord and causing him to be evicted from "their" home, when in reality, he still wasn't working and hadn't paid any rent in five months.

But, the most telling thing in Sam's letter is the lack of punctuation in his sentences. Sam ends what should have been a question with a period every time. He's not asking questions. *He's making statements*; a very subtle psychological attack on Bunny's conscience and emotions.

Bunny found letters on the seat of her car when she left work. Other letters had been mailed at the post office where she picked up her mail, and some of the earlier letters had been mailed in Lambertville, a 45-minute drive for Sam.

And then Sam, with a background in electronics, the Sam who had ranted endlessly about the many ways he could kill his first wife, the Sam who claimed he could make a bomb with his eyes closed, sent a bizarre message telling Bunny to expect a package in four days.

Package to arrive in four days!
PACKAGE TO ARRIVE IN FOUR DAYS!
Package To Arrive In Four Days!
Package to arrive in four days!
PACKAGE to arrive in four days!
PACKAGE TO ARRIVE in four days!
Package to arrive **IN FOUR DAYS!**

Bunny suddenly realized that she was being stalked, and that her life was in danger.

CHAPTER 11

"Simple obsession" stalking, which accounts for up to 80% of all stalking cases, is one of the most dangerous situations a victim can find them self in. It is a crime that is closely linked to, and is in fact an extension of, domestic violence. This type of stalker can have a long history of abusive and/or violent behavior, and while they may not have a criminal record, they are the most dangerous and sometimes deadly type of stalker. (Douglas, 266)

It is his practiced violent and abusive behaviors while in the relationship, combined with his personal knowledge of the victim, that make this stalker much more dangerous. When he has been in a long-term relationship with the victim the stalker knows where she works, who her friends are, what her schedule is, where she lives, where she shops, and who she relies on for help. He knows everything about her, including what gets to her, what upsets her, and what frightens her. (Douglas, 267)

Sadly, many victims don't realize that simply ending the relationship, moving or changing the locks isn't enough to end the violence. Most simple-obsession stalkers, the abusers who are out to get their former intimates one way or another, don't back off with the threat of criminal punishment. In fact, one third of the domestic violence victims in Lambertville had restraining orders against their abusers at the time they were assaulted. (LPD, 1996).

- One out of every twelve women and one out of every forty-five men in the United States have been stalked. (AP, 1997)
- 1,006,970 women and 370,992 men are stalked each year in the United States. (AP, 1997)
- Hunterdon County had 353 reported stalking incidents in 1996. (NJSP, 1996)

- There were two domestic violence-stalking cases in Lambertville in 1996. (LPD, 1996)
- 80 percent of the women who are stalked are assaulted by their stalker. (AP, 1997) Others are harassed verbally, in writing, or by phone.
- There were 30,191 reported domestic violence harassment incidents in Hunterdon County in 1996. (NJSP, 1996)
- Some stalkers follow their victims, laying in wait for them. Some stalkers vandalize their victim's property, home, or cars. Some stalkers kill the victim's pets.
- Lambertville had four cases of domestic violence related property damage in 1996. (LPD, 1996)
- There were over 6,300 reported domestic violence incidents of criminal mischief, burglary, and criminal trespassing in Hunterdon County in 1996. (NJSP, 1996)
- In Hunterdon County, there were 27 false imprisonments, 22 kidnappings, and 176 sexual assaults associated with domestic violence. (NJSP, 1996)
- And some abusers and stalkers murder.

To many, the threat of losing their homes, jobs, and other relationships due to arrests and convictions for violence and stalking isn't a real possibility. They have gotten away with domestic violence for so long that even the threat of police intervention isn't a reality to them. And, when the police are called, they just get angrier. In the abuser's mind, he perceives the stalking and harassment as being the victim's personal problem. In no way does he perceive any of this to be his problem, and he resents the police intervention. He feels his victim is being disloyal and causing him more problems. She has disobeyed him and is now harassing him with the police, even though it is he who has used all his skills to manipulate her, made plays on her sympathies, taken advantage of her vulnerability and inexperience and holds her directly responsible for his problems with the law. (Douglas, 279) There aren't any words to describe the rage he's feeling inside at this point.

As Douglas says, "Whether he's a sadistic serial killer who tortures and rapes children because he enjoys it, or a repeat domestic abuser who takes out his problems on the women in his life, he does what he does because it's who he is, and you won't be able to talk him out of it. On the contrary, if you are his victim, just by making yourself accessible to him you've given him a victory: he's regained a measure of control." (Douglas, 280)

*   *   *

Suzi was subject to stalking after she left Bill. She said, "One time, he was trying to climb the telephone pole at 4 a.m. to try and tap my phone. His friends said he was really messed up (on heroin) that night."

Bill followed Suzi everywhere. She saw him waiting for her after work, he appeared at the store when she went shopping, tried to go through her purchases, and she even saw him drive by every time she went to visit friends.

Bill cornered Suzi at work, repeatedly forcing her into an isolated area to try to intimidate her into sex, or forcing her to take drug tests, anything that he could do to upset her and keep her off balance. He knew she couldn't make a scene, because she might lose her job.

Bill took Suzi's mail from her mailbox and read it; and he intercepted her e-mail. He repeatedly phoned her at all hours of the day and night, and sabotaged her car.

Suzi finally took her daughter and fled across the country to escape the stalking. Bill tracked her down and forced her to return, and even tried to have her arrested for kidnapping.

He's still harassing her and doing everything he can do to make her life miserable, and although Suzi has since involved the police, Bill hasn't stepped far enough over the line to be arrested.

*   *   *

Bunny felt real fear after she received the bizarre note from Sam telling her she would receive a package in four days. If the promised package carried a bomb as she suspected, it meant that Sam intended to kill her.

She called the police. Over the next twelve hours, Bunny spoke with postal inspectors, special UPS and FedEx agents, coworkers, and family.

Arrangements were made to intercept and x-ray every package of the thousands that arrived at her place of employment on a daily basis. Every package addressed to her personally that could be delivered to any individual post office or through FedEx or UPS would be intercepted and x-rayed.

The post offices and delivery services of friends and family members who might accept a package for her were put on alert. Police departments in each municipality were notified.

Bunny made arrangements to have her car and apartment kept under 24-hour surveillance. She had an escort everywhere she went.

The promised package arrived four days later. It contained a few trinkets and a note from Sam telling Bunny he was sure she would appreciate the enclosed keepsakes of their marriage.

Much relieved, Bunny became even more determined never see or speak to Sam again and to follow through on her divorce plans as soon as possible.

Her lawyer sent a letter of intent to Sam. Sam fired back with death threats against the lawyer and any law enforcement officer who tried to serve him with divorce papers. Months later, the lawyer was still getting anonymous death threats in the mail.

Bunny received phone call after phone call from Sam. She hung up without speaking each time.

Then, Bunny received another letter.

Dear Bernadette,

I just can't believe that you still have a need to torment and show such cruelty towards me when I have shown you nothing but love. I stay out of your way, I don't bother or harass you in any way shape or form and each time I think I'm doing the correct thing you attack me again with your cruelty.

... I don't know what you are anymore, Bernadette; I only know that whatever it is has nothing to do with humanitarianism ...

... Sweetheart, there are things on my mind and in my heart that I must get out. We both agree that we are deeply in love with each other but why can't you say the words that you "love me." Honey, if there is one thing that I now know for sure it is that ... you [are] just a cruel person. I believe that you just don't see this cruelty in yourself; at least I need to believe that you don't, because if you are aware that you are being cruel to me and doing the things that you are doing to me, on purpose, then I never want to see or hear from you again!

I will continue this letter with the premise that you are unaware of your cruelty and do truly want to work at putting our marriage back to a place that will be much better and bring us much happiness for the rest of our lives.

Bernadette, we're both adults, and the time for playing games with me is over ... If you are getting some kind of pleasure out of coming back into my life and hurting me more, I want you to know that the only person you are truly hurting is yourself because I won't allow you to hurt me and you will just be depriving yourself of what you know is the greatest love affair of your life. Do you really want to throw away the last chance of gaining back the greatest love affair that either of us have ever known?

... I realize that right now I am a million light years ahead of where you are but it is you who must also be aware of that fact. I can see that you are stuck in the same place that you were in [when you left]. You have a lot of catching up to do to get where I am. With the right kind of help you will get there.

. . . I will no longer be the only giver in our relationship and what I mean is that I will also take. I spent years giving while everyone else took from me and what did all that giving, that came from my very heart and soul, get me?

It begot me the loss of my family and the loss of everyone and everything that I loved and it left me stuck with paying off other people's bills! I think you'll agree that it's time that I stop giving. One other thing that I expect is an apology from everyone who has made up the lies that I have had to endure during this whole affair.

There are many things that I have the right to be bitter about because of what was done to me. I owe no one any apology . . .

Honey, I know our love can work and that is because of where I am at.

You have to have the trust in me or nothing will work. This Sunday is Mother's Day, a day when husband and wife and their family should be together but because of the way you have already acted towards me, because of your cruelty, I know that you won't even have the common courtesy to see me, I've sent you a Mother's Day card anyway because I love you number one and because I have the courtesy and decency that are currently lacking in you.

Love,

Sam

P.S. Have a wonderful Mother's Day!

Sam seems to have gone full circle with this halfhearted, last-ditch attempt to regain control, and this letter is a good example of the fantasy world that Sam has created in his mind.

He perceives himself to be the kind, loving, caring partner in the relationship, the person who gave his all in an effort to keep the family together. He perceives the breakup of their marriage as Bunny's fault and blames her for his losing "everyone and everything." Rather than showing remorse and accepting responsibility for his actions towards Bunny, he perceives himself to be the victim. He has dismissed the fact that Bunny paid the rent, utility, and telephone bills for a full two months after she left and that the over $100,000 in purchases that were charged to his twenty-two individual charge accounts were made by him only.

We can see that Sam's state of mind has him believing that he is well adjusted and in full control of his life. If only Bunny would trust herself to him. He and only he can help her get over her personality flaws and cruelty. Sam is living in a state of *distorted thinking.*

Bunny was lucky. She's still waiting for her divorce to become finalized, and she hasn't heard from Sam in over a year. As some stalkers do, Sam moved on. Hopefully.

CHAPTER 12

Other victims aren't so lucky. The simple-obsession stalker has one objective, and that is to get his victim back in his life. When he finds that he's losing, he may switch his thinking around and decide to go for the ultimate act of control and punishment-murder.

Some victims are killed before they ever have the chance to leave the relationship. The statistics compiled by the Department of Justice on domestic murder present a frightening picture of the ultimate act of domestic violence. (1998)

- 1,800 people will be murdered by their intimate this year.
- 30% of all female murder victims and 3% of all male murder victims were killed by their spouse or intimate.
- 75% of women who are murdered by their abusive partners are killed either while they are attempting to leave or shortly after they left.

There have only been hints at the domestic violence that underscored Phil Hartman's marriage. What is known about the events leading up to the May 28, 1998 murder/suicide, is that the ten year marriage between Hartman and his wife, Brynn, was a troubled one, with Brynn the volatile and "erratic" partner. People Online (1998) reported that Hartman, a popular outgoing and talented performer, retreated into himself when he was home. The couple fought and argued frequently, with Brynn, an alcoholic and cocaine user, instigating the fights. Hartman would then withdraw to his bedroom. Hartman was quoted as saying, "I go into my cave and she throws grenades to get me out." (2) The violence ended when Brynn took a .38-caliber handgun and shot Hartman three times before killing herself.

Douglas states that the high rate of murder-suicides in simple-obsession stalking is because once the abuser has killed his victim, he has "no where else to go emotionally." (281) He goes on to say that the abusive partner who kills is unable to form and maintain normal emotional relationships. They see the violence and themselves in a slanted light, blaming the victim for their behavior. In reality, all of the experts agree, the abusers are cowardly, insecure, paranoid individuals who lack self-control and are unable to deal with their emotions. They suffer from a personality defect that distorts their thinking and shapes the course of their lives. It drives them to commit battery and murder.

In June 1995, Charles Trice Jr. was found guilty of first-degree murder in the death of his estranged wife, Darla. Trice, a former Florida state trooper, was an abuser who had threatened to kill his wife on numerous occasions. While out on $30,000 bail following an arrest for spousal abuse, Trice shot and killed Darla. He was found guilty of first-degree murder, burglary with an assault or battery and violation of a domestic violence order and sentenced to a mandatory life sentence. (Court, Florida v. Trice, 6/95)

In October 1993, Osby Jackson went looking for his estranged wife, Orrie. Jackson had been arrested three weeks earlier after threatening to kill Orrie. He told police at that time, that he was going to kill her as soon as he got out of jail and the police couldn't stop him. On the night of October 23, Jackson wound up at the home of Orrie's boyfriend, Greg Bailey at 2:00 a.m. When there was no answer at the door, Jackson broke into the house and confronted Bailey. As things escalated, a roommate ran to call the police while Bailey grabbed a cane and Jackson went into the kitchen to grab a butcher knife. When police arrived at the scene, Greg Bailey was dead. He had been stabbed eight times. Bailey had initially been stabbed in the kitchen. He had tried to get away from his attacker, but Jackson had chased him about fifty yards into a field before catching him and stabbing him again. Orrie was found dead in the hall, just outside the bedroom. She had been stabbed 19 times. Jackson told police at the time of his arrest, that he had no reason to live. He was found guilty of malice murders, burglary, and making terroristic threats and was sentenced to life in prison with no chance of parole in March 1997. (Court, Georgia v. Jackson, 3/97)

*   *   *

The problem of domestic violence isn't a social one, although it reaches out to touch our lives in many different ways. It is a problem that begins, for an unknown reason, deep within the mind of the abuser. It spreads from there, latching onto the first susceptible victim with its talons of dominance, control, and abuse.

The victims, due to their own inner makeup, are reluctant to break away. They intensely believe in the sanctity of marriage and the ideal of family and home. They want only to please, be accepted, and loved. And as the relationship deepens, the victim tends to accept the blame, feeling it is something they did to provoke their mate.

The first time they are hit, they want to believe that it will never happen again, and so, they try harder to please, to do what is wanted. As the abuse continues, they tend to accept the responsibility for their abuser's behavior, make excuses for it, and cover it up, at first unwilling, and then unable to walk away from what they hold so dear.

They are, in fact, perfect victims; and because of the type of person they are, they actually enable the batterer to continue in his cycle of abusive behavior. The victims are then propelled ever downward until they are stripped of their very being. And, for the victim, there is no easy way out; for once they realize what has happened, they have been convinced that they are worthless, useless, and incapable of rejoining the human race.

The victims of domestic violence must rediscover who they are. They must understand that the abuse is not their fault. They have been chosen by their intimate to play a role in a fantasy world; and to their intimate they are nothing more than a puppet. Regardless of what has been drummed into them, they must accept the fact that they are a good person, a useful person, and a capable person. They are a strong person, because it takes a strong person to endure years of abuse and violence. They must realize that they can leave. And, they must summon up all of their strength for what lies ahead, because breaking the circle of violence won't be easy. They will need to be stronger than they have ever been in their life, and take the reins of control within their own hands.

They will be at the mercy of an adversary who has practiced his predatory and manipulative skills far longer than they have been free. The victim will become a target for harassment, stalking, vandalism, manipulation, and even murder. It might be a long journey to freedom. They might have to disappear entirely to begin life anew. But, it can be done.

The first step is a phone call. To 9-1-1, if it's an emergency, otherwise, call the local police department or a local or national abuse hot line. The people who answer the phone will help. All the victim has to do is make the call. Everything else will fall in place. And, with time, will come healing.

The domestic violence support system can help, and must help all victims, regardless if they are male, female, heterosexual, or homosexual. Domestic violence laws and regulations must be modified to make it easier for victims to get the help they need. No one should have to confess to a crime in order to obtain protective shelter, and no one should be turned away because they are male. Domestic violence is a crime, with real offenders and real victims. Society has an obligation to make things as easy as possible for the victims, not harder.

And the abusers? Stiffer penalties for domestic violence offenses. Recognize the crimes for what they really are, and send the clear message that domestic violence will not be tolerated on any level. Put him in jail and leave him there. He knows what he did, and in fact, he did it on purpose-he deserves to be punished to the fullest extent of the law.

CHAPTER 13

Suddenly, the abusive relationship is over. The victim has found the strength and means to leave the violence and a bright beautiful world lies ahead of them, a world full of new relationships waiting to be discovered, stress-free, non-abusive lives and happy endings. In a perfect world, this would be true, but for the victims of domestic violence, the endings aren't always happy and life after the abuse can be difficult.

The victims who shared their stories of abuse here tell about their struggles to leave their abusive relationships and the major hurdles they had to overcome to live on their own without abuse. Other victims, who also wanted to share their stories, spoke candidly, with the desire of giving hope and encouragement to the men and women who are currently in abusive relationships. Those former victims, who have found happiness in new relationships, brought to their new relationships the emotional scars of domestic abuse. For the partners of the abused, the hardest part has been gaining trust while offering the emotional support that may still be needed many years down the road. They were all interviewed in the beginning of September (1998).

The victims told of serious depressions that lasted for years and the resulting hospitalizations, suicide attempts, alcoholism, mental health problems, and chronic fatigue that followed in the wake of their leaving. They told of severe panic attacks that lasted for months after escaping their abusers, attacks that would strike without warning, leaving them shaking and crying, their hearts racing. Others couldn't go near their old neighborhoods without suffering severe reactions that left them trembling and in tears. Despite the challenges to their emotional well-being, financial hardships, and a multitude of other problems they were faced with, not one victim ever considered giving up and going back to their abuser.

*   *   *

Sally, who has remained single, never found out that Alex was sexually abusing her children until several years after she left him. She is angry as she speaks of the emotional damage that was done to them by her former husband, and tells of putting the welfare of her children above her own emotional needs, and the resulting toll it took on her.

"When one of my children started displaying violent behavior, became verbally abusive and started lying, I started him in counseling," she said. "At one point the therapist insisted that I bring all my children to the sessions and at the first session with all of us, the bombshell about the sexual abuse was dropped. It turned out that Alex had been sexually abusing the children when I was out of the house. Even though I hated Alex with a passion, it took me over six months to fully believe and comprehend that he could have done this to our children. When my child eventually confronted him with this, he said 'The past is the past, forget about it.'

"At that time," Sally continued, "there was a statute of limitations that stopped us from prosecuting Alex. I wish he had gone to jail for the rest of his life. Fortunately, my other children were too young at the time of the abuse to remember it.

"I wound up feeling guilty about what happened to my children because even though I didn't know about the sexual abuse, I felt I should have known," she said. "As a result, I tried to become super mom, and between trying to juggle work, be a single parent, involvement in school activities and counseling appointments, I burned out. It took me a long time to recover to the point that I felt that I was a rational, independent person."

*   *   *

Lynn, who took her child and left Matt, spoke candidly about her depression and her struggle for freedom.

"At some point," she said, "I think I realized that I was probably going to wind up in Carrier Clinic or Trenton Psychiatric, long term. I had been fighting serious depression for a long time as a result of the verbal and mental abuse; I was alone, with no family in the area to turn to, and had resigned myself to being trapped in the relationship. It had taken ten years, but he had finally alienated me from all my friends and had convinced me that I was worthless and useless, incapable of doing anything 'properly' or on my own. Emotionally, I hit bottom.

"One day," Lynn continued, "he pushed the wrong button. As I walked in the door he accused me, as he had many times before, of having an affair and being out with a boyfriend. The issue was so stupid, because he knew where I had been, and he could have checked up on me at any time, but instead, he chose to make accusations.

"All of a sudden," she said, "I saw everything clearly, and in its proper perspective. I realized that it wasn't me who was the problem, it was him. My priority became my survival so that I could become well enough and strong enough to leave him and support my child and myself. For me, it wasn't just a case of having to leave the abusive situation, but of finding myself again and restoring my self-confidence so that I could leave.

"Looking back on it," Lynn said, "I think what I did took a lot of guts. I stood up to him at every turn. I started secretly saving every penny that I could get my hands on and then I took out a loan, bought a used car, and got my own insurance. I took my time and found a good job that offered a lot of security.

"Naturally," Lynn continued, "he thought it was a stupid job that any idiot could do. He really tried to get me to quit, but I stood up to him. When he refused to watch our child, I found a babysitter. I opened my own checking account. Every day, I got stronger. I ignored him and refused to get caught up in his mind control games. I told him I was leaving after I found a place to live and all of my plans were in place. It took me nearly three years from the time I decided to leave until I said, 'See ya!'

"It was probably the hardest thing I'll ever have to do in my life," Lynn said of her struggle to leave Matt, "and the three years between when I decided to leave and when I was actually able to leave, were a constant battle of wits and wills, but I focused on the freedom that was waiting at the end of the road.

"My first night out of the house was heaven," she said. "I just kept thinking over and over, 'I did it! I'm free.' At that point, I had my child, a good job, a new car, and a place to live. I was on cloud 9!

"Even after I left," she continued, "he did everything he could to make my life miserable. He would only take our child on my days off even if he wasn't working, forcing me to spend over half my salary on babysitters. He'd take the child on a vacation and come back the next day, drop the child off at the babysitter's and not even tell me. Anything he could do to screw things up for me seemed to be fair game. I quickly learned that I could only rely on myself, because his promises were as empty as they had always been. It was a constant struggle for a couple of years to make ends meet and juggle my work schedule with that of the babysitter, but we survived.

"The one thing I didn't want any part of was men," Lynn recalled. "I wasn't willing to take a chance on another relationship. But, when I met my husband a few months later, I knew instantly that I was going to have to rethink my ideas. He's the exact opposite of my 'ex;' a kind, gentle, man who makes me feel like a queen. In his eyes, there's nothing I can't accomplish. He loves me, thinks I'm beautiful, loves my cooking, and is my biggest supporter. He'll never know how deeply I love him or how complete and wonderful my life is with him beside me. Those are things I can't begin to explain."

Scott, Lynn's husband, said, " Lynn still won't wear a sleeveless blouse because she thinks she looks fat. That's a carryover from her abusive relationship. She's not fat–she's sexy and beautiful. He downed her all the time; she couldn't get a job, she couldn't cook or do anything right. He gave her no support.

"She still goes into a closet when it comes to sports," Scott continued. "He not only loved sports, but he gambled. I can't even get her to watch a ball game–she totally shuts down.

"When I first met her, she was very insecure and backward with people she didn't know. She never wanted to speak in public or be in any groups. That was from the abuse, too, because he constantly put her down. She's come out of it very gradually. It wasn't until she was fifty years old that she said she wanted to do something that she had wanted to do her entire life. Now, she's doing it and she's very happy.

"I think the abuse and its aftermath made her strong," Scott said. "There's nothing she can't do. And, through her strength, she's made me a stronger person."

*   *   *

Bunny, who was stalked after she left her husband Sam, shows no signs of the fear she displayed in 1998. The letters, phone calls, and threats from Sam stopped when Sam suddenly disappeared. Bunny hired a private detective, enlisted the help of a "people finder" service, and even reported him as a missing person to the police-not because she wanted to resume communications with him, but because she wanted to serve him with divorce papers. Despite her efforts, no one has seen or heard from Sam since he disappeared. If, as she believes, Sam finally carried through on his threats to commit suicide, his body has never been found.

"Timing is everything," said Bunny. "I believe God would not hand me more than I could deal with. Even though I was emotionally beaten by Sam, I believe I have a lot of strength. As far as I'm concerned, Sam hung himself. I had even gone to counseling with him and I felt no guilt when I left. The timing was right as far as I'm concerned.

"Any woman waiting to leave an abusive relationship must

understand that what's ahead of her isn't as bad as what she's in now," she continued. "No victim should be afraid to ask for help from family, friends, or agencies. When you leave, you're living on adrenaline. I was lucky. I was able to move in with my sister, and another relative gave me $1000 towards an apartment.

"My biggest hurdle was being on my own financially for the first time in my life," Bunny said. "Even today, two years after I left Sam, I'm at least a month behind in half my bills, but at least I have my sanity, my life, and my children. And, being behind in your bills isn't the worst thing that could happen to someone. I'm busy enjoying my life and helping others and I donate a lot of volunteer time.

"I suffered from depression for quite a while after I left Sam," she continued. "My therapist said it was similar to post traumatic stress syndrome. For a year and a half, I didn't stop looking over my shoulder everywhere I went. I was afraid that Sam would show up at my apartment or at work. There was stalking and written intimidation, but I was always leery of up close personal contact. Knowing his state of mind and that he couldn't be trusted, I was afraid he might try to hurt me or want revenge.

"For the first six months I was on my own," Bunny said, "I had vivid nightmares where I could hear his voice and see him in the bedroom with me. I could hear him talking outside my window and see him sitting on my bed, crying and threatening suicide. I knew it wasn't real, but it was so vivid and his voice was so clear . . .

"For a full year all I really wanted was uninterrupted sleep and total quiet. I couldn't even turn my TV on for six months because it reminded me of the way he used to sit in front of the set, drinking and neglecting the family. Visiting friends or relatives and hearing the clank of ice in a glass made my heart stop cold because it was an instant reminder of the beginning of Sam's nightly ritual. I used to pray for one night with no clanking of ice. I couldn't even buy an ice cube tray for a year.

"Throughout the abuse," she said, "I never forgot that I was

pretty or a good person, and I never lost my faith in God. I didn't
have any problems with my self-image, but for over a year I didn't
want to date or even meet anyone.

"I finally joined a church group to meet new friends," Bunny
continued. "I had enough confidence in myself that I knew I could
trust myself to stick to my rules if I met a man. I knew that I'd
never fall into the abusive trap again. I was looking for red flags;
looking at behavior patterns, seeing if people's actions went with
their words, listening to how men spoke of their former wives, and
seeing how they treated their children. I think these are all indications of how a man will treat a woman. I was maintaining my own
independence and was leery of falling into any traps where I'd
wind up dependent on someone else. While I wasn't opposed to
changes in the future that might have lead to a happy, non-abusive relationship, I wanted to maintain full control of things.

"I'm a firm believer that God had a hand in introducing me to
my boyfriend. It took me nine months or so before I was able to let
my guard down and trust him, to really understand that he would
never abuse me. He has proven to me that there are good, kind,
non-abusive people out there."

Bunny is still with her boyfriend. She's content with their
relationship and loves the positive attention she now gets. With
her divorce from Sam now final, she is hoping that a new, caring,
and loving marriage is in her future.

*   *   *

Today, Tippi is a self-assured woman who has been in a long-term
relationship. When she left A.H., she chose, unlike the other victims, to rely on public agencies for the help she needed. She still
speaks bitterly about the system that she feels failed both her and
her child.

"I was informed by the court system, mental health groups,
and my personal physician that there were outlets for help for
both single parents and their children," Tippi said. "But guess

what? You'd better either be dirt poor or filthy rich in order to get these services. If you happen to be in the medium income, these government agencies will eventually wipe you out financially. "After I left A.H.," she continued, "I tried to work through Social Services because I felt my child and I needed counseling so that both of our self esteems could be restored. I quickly found out that I made too much money to qualify for assistance or reduced rates. What average family can afford to pay $150 or more per session per week? It's really a shame that, no matter whether it's a man or a woman, if they're the custodial parent who is trying to provide a decent living for their family, they are penalized. I was finally able to find someone who accepted my medical insurance but my experience was that when you're the custodial parent and the so-called 'experts' know that the non-custodial parent is the cause of the problems, and you go to them for help, they can lower your self esteem even more by telling you that you're not doing enough for your family.

"What I finally concluded was that without the support of family and friends and a damn good sense of humor, I wouldn't be the self-supporting self-efficient person that I am today," she said. "The more you go through, the stronger you become. I guess by now, I'm super woman!"

CHAPTER 14

Jessica, another victim of domestic violence, complains about the twenty-five plus pounds she has gained in the last two months. She's been fighting weight problems for years and blames the depression that came from the mental and physical abuse she suffered at the hands of her "ex."

"I met John in a store when I was not quite 21," she said. "He was so handsome that I fell in love with him instantly. Within months, we were living together and a baby was on the way.

"Things started going wrong right away," she continued. "I found out he was an alcoholic. All through my pregnancy, I got choked, beat, had knives pulled on me. He made me go through the pregnancy all by myself, and just dropped me off at the curb when I went into labor. After my daughter was born, he started accusing me of running on him.

"One time," Jessica continued, "I went to buy an ice cream cone and he accused me of sleeping with the ice cream man. He dumped a bottle of wine on my head that night. One night, I forgot to bring the garlic salt to the table and he dumped the whole bowl of spaghetti on my head and my daughter's head. My daughter was only two at the time. By the time she was four, he was telling her to call me a 'bitch' and encouraging her to slap me in the face. If I tried to discipline her, he would hit me. Around that time, he gave her a gun and told her to shoot me.

"I was hit, locked in the house, isolated and threatened every day for nearly ten years," she said. "He'd beat me up and then demand sex. One day, I came to Lambertville to visit a friend and never went home again. I stayed with my friend, sleeping on the living room floor with my daughter for a year and a half before I was able to get my own apartment.

"I was drinking heavily at that point," Jessica continued. "My daughter was in school, and I went out and found a job. I couldn't afford a babysitter. I was fortunate that my boss allowed my daughter to stay with me at work after school. It was really hard. My depression was really bad. I wound up on anti-depressants and washing them down with alcohol. Then I met Dave.

"To this day, I don't know what attracted me to him," she said. We started dating and within a month, he started abusing me. He came over one night and I had gotten a bottle of wine out for us. He took one look at the bottle and called me a 'fucking lush.' Then he threw me on the floor and kicked me in the head with his boots. I immediately ended the relationship.

"As soon as I broke it off, he started stalking me," Jessica said. "He'd break into my apartment and turn all the lights on so when I got home I'd know he'd been there. I changed the locks. He constantly drove by my house and phoned at least ten times a day.

"One day, when he called, I slammed the phone down on him and he came after me," she continued. "I ran over to my friend Todd's house for protection. Todd had been a good friend since the day I met him and he had always supported me emotionally. He was really concerned for my safety and so he took me home and spent the night with me, alert to every sound. We wound up spending many nights sitting up and talking about me and my problems.

"Dave finally tapered off and left me alone," Jessica said. "Todd and I realized almost immediately that our friendship would bond us together forever. We've been together for fifteen years and I'm more content than I've been in my whole life. Todd has told me many times that he'd die for me. He protects me and looks out for me. My daughter thinks of Todd as her father. For the first time in my life, I finally feel safe."

"When I first met Jessica," Todd said, "she was very confused and scared. I saw a hurt person who was crying out for help. No matter what I said to her, she didn't believe me. She couldn't accept a compliment. But, I saw someone who had a very big heart and I turned the key. She did the rest. I wanted to make her feel wanted and help build her self-esteem.

"The biggest part was getting her to trust me," he continued. For a person who was not abused to be with a person who was abused, takes a lot of perseverance and patience. I had a lot to do to build her trust and self esteem. After fifteen years, we've built a solid relationship based on friendship, dedication, mutual respect, understanding, sharing each others' feelings, and love.

"It wasn't always easy," Todd said of his relationship with Jessica. "Jessica was drinking heavily when we first started living together. I hid the bottles, dumped bottles of alcohol down the drain, spoke with the pharmacist about her pills. I did everything I could to help her and make her feel good about herself. She sees the doctor on a regular basis now and has quit drinking. She's still fighting her self-image, though. She gets upset when the doctor's scale shows a four-pound difference from the month before. Her weight doesn't bother me. She's beautiful on the inside and out."

"I think my overeating is a form of self-abuse," Jessica said. "Domestic violence changes your character and the way you see things forever. I don't know why I overeat."

"I think," Todd added, "that it's her way of compensating for the years of emotional and physical abuse. She could weigh 300 pounds, and I'd still love her."

*   *   *

Molly came from a mentally and psychologically abusive relationship that turned physically abusive. While her husband, Randy, wasn't as verbal in telling Molly that he thought she was stupid or incompetent as some of our other abusers, he tended to talk admirably about other women.

Molly was also luckier than many other victims when it was

time to leave. She had a good part time job that became full time and she was able to rent a house within days of leaving Randy.

"When you listened to him talk about other women," Molly said, "he made them sound sharp and interesting in comparison to me being the dowdy homebody. When I had my son, he made me feel that I was a blimp. He'd say I was ungrateful for having him as a partner. He always told me about the older women he knew who were so appreciative of him and who stroked his ego.

"The first time I was hit," she said, "we had only been married a year and a half. I was pregnant, and we had made plans for New Year's Eve. He didn't like the plans that we had made, so he punched me and left a huge bruise on my leg. The physical abuse continued sporadically after that" although, she added, "he didn't hit me every time we had a fight.

"Once," she continued, "after we had been married five years, we were down at the shore and had made plans to do something with his family. He decided to go golfing instead, and I was really disappointed. So, I ran out to the car and asked him to change his mind. I must have leaned into the car a little, because he rolled the window up on my arm and stepped on the gas. He dragged me and ran over my foot with the car. He injured me pretty badly.

"I realized at some point that I was nothing to him," Molly said. "He was abusing me and talking about all the 'babes' he knew at work. While he had a string of girlfriends that he was seeing, I was just the old lady at home.

"I was afraid he was going to give me AIDS or something like that," she continued, "and I knew there must be something more to life. Even though he was making me feel inferior and making it appear that he was the strong one, in reality, I was giving him his strength and he was actually the weak one.

"When I told him I wanted a divorce, he told me I'd better watch everything I ate, be careful when I started my car, and that he'd put me in a coffin," Molly recalled. "I took my son and left with nothing but the clothes on my back and a small amount of money in my pocket. He was full of revenge and even stole my car on a holiday weekend.

"He had another girlfriend within days of my leaving," she continued. "He got his just dues when she gave him a venereal disease. Randy has continued to have a constant string of girl-friends. Many of them are physically abusive themselves. I was always afraid that my son would wind up in the middle of a fight or that one of their former boyfriends would come after them and hurt my child. I even gave my son instructions not to get involved in anything. I told him, get out, go to a neighbor's-it's not your fight, it's theirs.

"After I left Randy," Molly continued, "I spent a lot of time in a dance club with my friends. For me it was a way of escaping while having fun and meeting new people.

"The biggest thing for me was that I realized I never had the love and comfort that married couples share. In an abusive situation, there is no love or comfort at any time during the relationship. I was looking for that love and the closeness, but I really didn't want to meet anyone because I felt that my judgment was impaired because I had married Randy, and I was afraid of making the same mistake again. Finding that one real person who can give you the love you need is hard. I found that there aren't that many wonderful people out there.

"I'm not sure if the feelings of trust and mistrust when you meet someone new are about the person you've just met or feelings of mistrust about yourself," Molly continued. "The first Christmas after I had met Carl, I was in my living room watching him and my son decorate the tree, and I said to myself, 'Who is this man?' We had been together six months and here he was, string-ing popcorn for the tree, a normal family thing, and I'm thinking that he could be a serial killer, or a child molester-just anybody. We spent a lot of time just sitting and talking before I finally felt secure."

"I listened to what Molly told me," said Carl, "and I realized that if there was ever anything she wanted to do, I would go along with it. Her former husband never did anything with her. On Friday nights he'd get home, and the first thing he'd do was refuse to eat her cooking. Then he'd just watch TV. On Saturdays and Sundays he played golf. They never did anything together.

"She started playing racquetball with her girlfriend," he continued, "and then she'd go out to a club for a drink afterward. Randy would always have something for her to do, anything he could think of to disrupt her routine, to keep her from going out.

"When her divorce was going through," Carl continued, "she'd get letters in the mail from her lawyer, updating the status. It would bother her for a day or more. I would always dread seeing that letter in the mail. She'd be angry and just keep letting it out, and it would upset whatever we had planned. Her whole mood would be disrupted.

"Everything Randy wanted to do always came first," he said. "What Molly wanted to do always came second, or they just wouldn't do it. Just this week we had to go out of town on business. On the way, Molly saw a billboard for Atlantic City and thought that would be fun to do on the way home. It was out of our way, but at 10 o'clock at night, we were standing on the beach. We went to the casinos and played the machines. It's important to share in what each other wants to do. That's more interesting than being so selfish."

"I think domestic violence does make you tremendously strong," Molly said. "Because you've left once, you know that you will never have to put up with abuse again and you know you'll have the strength to leave at the first signs of any abuse in the future. No one should put up with it."

*   *   *

The victims who told their stories and shared their experiences here all want to send a message to anyone currently trapped in an abusive situation:

Leave now. Domestic violence is the worst thing that has or

will happen to you. What you'll go through after you leave your abuser may be hard, but you won't be the first person or the only person who has gone through it. You may have problems with depression or adjustment and it may be hard to find a job or a place to live, but everything will work out. No matter how hard it might be, and no matter how many problems you might have to face on your own, it will be a better life and easier on you and your children than what you endured in the abusive relationship. You are not stupid, ugly, or incompetent; but you are a very strong person, and, you'll make it on your own in a new life without domestic violence.

We all went through what you're going through, and we all made it.

CHAPTER 15

This look at domestic violence has taken us from the darkest moments in the lives of several Lambertville women to the police officer on the beat and finally into the irrational mind of the abuser. And in the end, we have exposed the abuser for the weak, incompetent coward he is.

As this book draws to a close, I'd like to share some final thoughts.

The response I got from "In the Name of Love," the original newspaper series published in The Beacon, was overwhelming. In addition to winning the first place Lloyd P. Burns Memorial Award in the 1998 New Jersey Press Association Better Newspaper Contest, (Editorial Competition, for Responsible Journalism in the area of Public Service, for a weekly newspaper with under 4,500 readers), I have been asked to make guest appearances and speak about domestic violence. I have made countless copies of the series for friends and family and am always asked to publish the series as a book so that more victims of domestic violence will have access to this information.

Copies of the original study have been placed in organizations across the country ranging from the Lambertville Police Department to the Pierce County Domestic Violence Commission in Tacoma, WA.

Friends and strangers alike have stopped me on the street or called to tell me their stories of abuse. I was even stopped on the boardwalk in Wildwood, NJ by a friend who just wanted to tell me how much her mother enjoyed the series.

And I have heard of more abuse; men who kept birth certificates, driver's licenses, and other personal papers of their victims with them at all times in an effort to control, who disconnected phones to prevent communications with friends and family, and who have subjected their victims to senseless beatings and unbelievable mental cruelty.

More importantly, I have seen how the series has touched lives and turned them around for the better. Three women contacted me to share their stories after reading the series and recognizing the signs of abuse in their daughters' relationships.

All three passed the newspaper series along to their daughters who were living in various parts of the country in the hopes they would read the series and understand what was happening in their lives.

One daughter, after a few weeks, called her mother and said, "Come get me."

The second young woman is also back home with her mother after taking her baby and walking out on her drug addicted abusive husband. She simply didn't go home one day. She is now fighting the stalking and harassment that followed her leaving, but she is determined not to give in.

Before the third woman was able to get out of her situation, her abuser found out about her plans to leave. In a rage, he went after her with a weapon, determined to kill her rather than let her leave. Within minutes of a frantic call from her father in Lambertville to the local police in her mid-western town, the daughter was safely removed from the deadly situation. She's now home with her parents and adjusting to a life without violence.

Along with the good stories came the not so good. I have spoken with parents who, after reading the series and despite their best efforts, have daughters who continue to blame themselves for the abuse in their lives and were reluctant to leave their intimates. Another woman I spoke with left her abuser only to find herself victimized by another abuser before breaking the cycle.

And I have heard several stories of domestic violence affecting mothers and daughters with the cycle of abuse passing down through the generations.

Some stories have taken yet a different turn. I spoke with another woman who felt victimized not only by her former spouse, but the system that dragged its judiciary heels as she followed him from state to state and court to court trying to collect 18 years of back child support.

"For me," she said, "the abuse has continued on a different level."

In closing, I want to thank the former victims of domestic violence who shared their stories. These women openly spoke about segments of their lives that were sometimes so painful that they cried just remembering what they went through. They shared some of their deepest secrets and talked about acts of violence and abuse that had never been shared with anyone before.

It was the telling of these stories that gave others the wisdom to recognize the abuse in their own situations and the strength and courage to leave.

For them, I thank you.

WORKS CITED

- American Bar Association. Raphael & Tolman. *Trapped by Poverty, Trapped by Abuse: New Evidence Documenting the Relationship Between Domestic Violence and Welfare.* 1997. Available: http://www.abanet.org/domviol/stats.html 20 May 1998

- American Psychological Association. *Violence and the Family: Report of the American Psychological Association Presidential Task Force on Violence and the Family.*1996

- Associated Press. "Study: Stalking Widespread". 1997. Available: http://www.thonline.com/th/news/111697/ National/83846.htm. 3 June 1998

- Barnes. "It's Just a Quarrel." *American Bar Association Journal.* Feb. 1998.

- Boston University Medical Center. Community Outreach Health Information System. 1995-1996. Available: http:// web.bu.edu/COHIS/violence/. 19 May 1998.

- Brott, Armin A. The Washington Post. "When Women Abuse Men: It's Far More Widespread Than People Think". Special supplement. December 28, 1993. Available: http:// www.vix.com/pub/men/battery/damnabledenial.html. 6 May 1998.

- Court Library. Georgia v. Jackson. 3/97. Available: http:// www.courttv.com/casefiles/verdicts/jackson.html. 7 June 1998

- Court Library. Florida v. Trice. 6/95. Available: http:// www.courttv.com/casefiles/verdicts/trice.html. 7 June 1998

- Cleckley, Hervey, M.D. *The Mask of Sanity.* US: C.V. Mosby Co., 1988.

- Dawson, John & Patrick Langan. *Murder in Families.* Washington, D.C.:U.S. Department of Justice, Bureau of Justice Statistics. 1994
- Douglas, John and Olshaker, Mark. *Obsession.* NY: Simon & Schuster, 1998.
- Florida Governor's Task Force on Domestic and Sexual Violence. *Florida Monthly Review Project.* 1997
- Geberth, Vernon J. *Practical Homicide Investigation: Tactics, Procedures, and Forensic Techniques.* Third Edition. NY:CRC Press. 1996
- Hare, Robert D. *Without Conscience: The Disturbing World of the Psychopaths Among Us.* New York: Pocket Books, 1993.
- Holmes, Ronald M. and Holmes, Stephen T. *Profiling Violent Crimes.* 2nd Edition. Thousand Oaks, CA:Sage Publications, Inc. 1996
- Kramer, Sue W. Victim interviews. 1998.
- Lambertville Police Department. Domestic violence case files. 1996
- Lambertville Police Department. Domestic violence case files. 1998
- McLaughlin, William. Personal interview. 29 June 1998
- Metro Nashville Police Department. Domestic Violence Division. 1998. Available: http://www.nashville.net/~police/abuse/. 19 May 1998.
- Murphy. "Equal protection for Victims of Same-Sex Domestic Violence" *Queer Justice.* 30 Val.U. L. Rev. 335. 1995.
- NJ State Police. Uniform Crime Reporting Unit. *Crime in New Jersey.* State of New Jersey. 1996.
- Orloff et al. "With No Place to Turn: Improving Advocacy for Battered Immigrant Women". *Family Law Quarterly.* vol. 29, no. 2. Summer, 1995.
- People Online. "Beneath the Surface". 1998. Available: http://www.pathfinder.com/people/980615/features/cover.html.18 June 1998.

- Price, Joyce. The Washington Times. "Report is a Reminder Men are Battered Too." January31, 1994. Available: http://www.vix.com/pub/men/battery/damnabledenial.html. 6 May 1998.
- Rand, Michael. *Violence Related Injuries Treated in Hospital Emergency Departments.* Washington, D.C.: U.S. Department of Justice, Bureau of Justice Statistics. 1997.
- Rasche, Christine. "Given' Reason for Violence in Intimate Relationships". *Homicide: The Victim/Offender Connection.* Cincinnati: Anderson Publishing Company. 1993.
- Standard-Times Online. New Bedford, MA 1995. Available:http://www.s-t.com/projects/DomVio/. 6 May 1998.
- Turvey, Brent E. "Behavior Evidence: Understanding Motives and Developing Suspects in Unsolved Serial Rapes Through Behavioral profiling Techniques". June, 1996 Available: http://www.corpus-delicti.com/. 7 July 1998
- Turvey, Brent E. Criminal Profiling. A Knowledge Solutions Forensic Science Course. Course Notes. Available: http://www.corpus-delicti.com/. 20 March 1998.
- Turvey, Brent E. Personal interview via e-mail. 11 May 1998.
- Turvey, Brent E. Profiling and Psychopathy. A Knowledge Solutions Forensic Science Course. Course Notes. Available: http://www.corpus-delicti.com/. 29 May 1998.
- Turvey, Brent E. Serial Rape Investigation. A Knowledge Solutions Forensic Science Course. Course Notes. Available: http://www.corpus-delicti.com/. 7 July 1998.
- U.S. Department of Justice. Bureau of Justice Statistics. Washington, DC. 1997
- U.S. Department of Justice. Bureau of Justice Statistics. Press Release. "Murder by Intimates Declined 36 Percent Since 1976: Decrease Greater for Male Than for Female Victims". March 16, 1998.

- U.S. Department of Justice and Federal Bureau of Investigation. Uniform Crime Reports. *Law Enforcement Officers Killed and Assaulted.* 1996.
- Young, Cathy. *A Man's Life.* "Woman Trouble". 1998. Available: http://www.manslife.com/family/new_violence/cathy1.html. June 1998

Printed in the United Kingdom
by Lightning Source UK Ltd.
105125UKS00001B/21